ADOPTING YOUR CHILD

ADOPTING YOUR CHILD
Options, Answers, and Actions

Nancy Thalia Reynolds

Self-Counsel Press Inc.
a subsidiary of
International Self-Counsel Press Ltd.
Canada U.S.A.
(Printed in Canada)

Printed in Canada

First edition: October, 1993; Reprinted: March, 1994

Cataloging in Publication Data

Reynolds, Nancy Thalia
Adopting your child
(Self-counsel reference series)
ISBN 0-88908-295-2
1. Adoption — United States. 2. Adoption — Canada.
I. Title. II. Series.
HV875.55.R49 1993   362.7'34'0973 C93-091802-9

Cover photography by Terry Guscott, ATN Visuals, Vancouver, B.C.

Self-Counsel Press Inc.
a subsidiary of
International Self-Counsel Press Ltd.

1481 Charlotte Road	1704 N. State Street
North Vancouver, British Columbia	Bellingham, Washington
Canada V7J 1H1	98225

CONTENTS

TABLES

EXERCISES

CHECKLISTS

ACKNOWLEDGMENTS

Hundreds of people gave me the benefit of their time and expertise over the past eight months. Joan Ramos, of Children's Home Society, in Seattle, Washington, offered intelligent critique, feedback, directed me to resources, and challenged my asssumptions. Patricia Irwin Johnston reviewed the chapter on infertility and gave me useful feedback. Seattle counselor, Sally Graham, located resources on decision-making for me.

Many adoption agency staff took time to discuss agency policy and practice with me. I owe special thanks to Carol Hollar of Americans for International Aid and Adoption, Carol Ryan of Catholic Children's Services, Judith Secord of New Hope, Jim Pahz of Children's Hope, Jane Gilbert of Open Door, Lillian Thorgerson of WACAP, and Forrest Wilton of Adoptive Parents' Association of British Columbia, who took the time to answer many questions.

Albert Lirhus responded to off-the-wall legal questions with aplomb, and Cora White answered many exacting questions on foster care. Susan Madsen answered or tracked down experts to answer questions about child protective services, and Alice Madsen shared what she learned during the five months she and her husband spent in Brazil adopting two children. Finally, I thank my mother, Eva, and my husband, Michael, and children, Nicholas and Emily, for the priceless gift of time and space in which to write.

INTRODUCTION

a. WHY THIS BOOK WAS WRITTEN

This is the book I wish someone had given to me when I first looked into adoption. It was conceived to help would-be adoptive parents acquire the skills they need to advocate for themselves, work through the chaotic and confusing adoption "system," and come out on the other side as successful parents.

When my husband and I began to explore adoption as a way of building our family, I pictured a simple, straightforward process. I knew it could take a year or more from the time we signed on with an agency until we had our baby and that there would be plenty of frustrations along the way. But if we were patient, I thought, one day the magic phone call would come from our agency telling us "your baby is ready for you." My mental picture couldn't have been further from the way it really happened — or usually happens.

Two years after we started, we were indeed adoptive parents, but of a baby adopted independently from Brazil, without agency help. While we were thrilled with the final results, we found ourselves following many aggravating, expensive, and unnecessary dead ends before we got there. Although we sought and received help from a succession of agencies, in the end we found our baby through networking with other adoptive parents. Over the two years, I frequently drew on my legal and advocacy experience to help us out, and I often wondered how adoptive parents managed who didn't have my background.

Perhaps the biggest surprise of all was that few agencies saw my family as their client. Most agencies perceive their role to be finding parents for their child clients, and it's not hard to understand why. Today's agencies are swamped with difficult-to-place children with heart-wrenching histories who have become increasingly higher priorities. We did encounter some for-profit facilitators and agencies who represented adoptive parents, but the kinds of adoption they facilitated weren't what our family was looking for and, in any event, their fees were beyond our means.

The most important lesson I learned during those two years was this: would-be adoptive parents must learn to advocate for themselves. Yet, as a volunteer dispensing adoption information to the public, I find that most prospective adoptive families continue to have the same unrealistic expectations I once did.

My purpose is to help you understand how adoption works and how you can make yours happen. I won't tell you where you can find your child. Even if that were possible in theory, the fact is that the world of adoption changes almost daily. Every year, new adoption agencies come into existence and old ones fold. Information about which countries permit international adoptions would be out of date before this book reached its first reader. But information on how you can learn to navigate the system for yourself, understand your options, and develop a workable strategy for your adoption is more enduring, and my aim is to provide that here for you.

b. WHO THIS BOOK IS FOR

This book is for anyone who is considering adoption or has come to the decision to adopt. It can be used at any and all stages of the adoption process. If you are an infertile individual or couple, preferential adopters (people who can have or have already had biological children but would now like to adopt), stepparents seeking to adopt stepchildren, relatives seeking to adopt an extended family member such as a grandchild, or a Canadian interested in adopting in the United States, this book was written for you. Whether you plan to use an agency or adopt privately, and whatever kind of child you are considering, this book will offer information and concrete suggestions on how to proceed.

c. WHAT THIS BOOK WILL AND WON'T DO AND WHY

This book focuses on process; it's about getting from here to there. It's natural to want to start by deciding on the kind of child you hope to adopt and then figure out how to make the adoption happen. Many books about adoption start that way. This one doesn't. My experience, and that of other adoptive parents, is that factors beyond our control played a bigger part than we did in determining the kind of children we could adopt, not to mention when and how and at what cost. Also, many adoptive parents change their minds about the kind of child they want to adopt, sometimes more than once, as they work their way through the adoption process. These changes are not necessarily a result of having to give up a cherished dream in the face of adoption reality. Often, as we learn about adoption and the children who need homes, we find ourselves drawn to a different kind of child and parenting experience than we first envisioned.

This book will introduce you to the larger world of adoption and the options in it before discussing how to make your own adoption happen. It is a map of how to adopt, designed like a road atlas, showing the freeways, secondary routes, and all the places you'll have to go through to get to your child, even though they aren't your final destination. Too often the process of adopting is experienced as a nightmare from which adopting parents awaken only when they finally receive their child. This book aims to help parents make their adoption experience a positive one.

Chapter 1 describes the contradictory world of adoption and explains why as a would-be adoptive parent you need to become your own advocate. Chapters 2 and 3 offer a brief discussion of adoption laws, and an introduction to the people and institutions that populate the adoption landscape. Chapter 4 discusses infertility and adoption readiness. Chapter 5 explores the options open to you: where you fit in as prospective parents, what kinds of children can be adopted, and the different routes to adoption. Chapter 6 shows you how to set goals for your adoption experience, not just the obvious final outcome of a child, but short, interim, and process goals that can help you take control of the process and turn a difficult experience into a positive one.

Chapters 7, 8, 9, and 10 are about building an adoption strategy for agency, independent, stepparent, and relative adoptions. Chapter 11 discusses how Canadian citizens can adopt in or through the United States. Chapter 12 covers financial planning, troubleshooting, coping with stress, and planning for the big event. Chapter 13 is about becoming a new parent, and in chapter 14, the ways in which you can share your adoption experience with your community are explored.

At the end of each chapter is a Resource Guide to help you explore further. Adoption is subject to sudden changes of law and procedure. While some books have stood the test of time admirably, others have not. For that reason, I have selected resources carefully. A basic text that is revised frequently may serve the reader better than one that is five years out of date, however beautifully written. The Tips sections include ideas and leads for further investigation.

It would be impossible to put everything you need to know about adoption in one book and that is not my purpose here. But within yourself and scattered out there in the community are all the resources you'll need to make your adoption happen. My goal is to encourage and help you feel empowered to take charge of your adoption experience and find the people, groups, books, and other resources you'll need along the way.

Even when you choose an agency adoption, the experience is a lot like being your own midwife. Ultimately, it's the energy and commitment coming from you, through all the frustrations, delays, and endless paperwork, that will bring a new child into your life. I wish you good luck in your search and joy in your new family.

1
WELCOME TO THE WORLD OF ADOPTION

Every year, over 150,000 adoptions take place in the United States and Canada. About 1 in 50 people is adopted, and 20% of North American families are linked through adoption. We call adoption a "system" for want of a better term, but it's a poor description. "System" implies a coherent whole, with all parts related to each other. In reality, adoption is a set of independent, occasionally overlapping systems. No single agency or institution is responsible for all elements of an adoption. Rather, private agencies, local, state, and federal governments, the judicial system, as well as social workers and lawyers may each play a role. The more complex scenario of international adoption also involves the other country's local, state, and federal governments along with orphanage staff, lawyers, translators, and interpreters.

Within the adoption process, separate players function independently. An adoption agency has no power over a judge; an adoption attorney cannot tell a social worker what to write in a home study (a pre-placement report on the adoptive family, which is required by law prior to an adoption). In fact, only one party to adoption links every element of the process: you. The ease or difficulty of the process and its outcome are, finally, your responsibility. No one else involved in your adoption will be there each step of the way to provide continuity and to take charge. If you don't accept the challenge of managing your own adoption, no one else will. The good news is that the resources you need to take control exist right now in your community; ways to access them are set out in this book.

a. SOME STARTING ASSUMPTIONS

1. Adoptive families are different from birth families

It's easy to understand that there is a difference between adopting and bearing biological children. But once the child is in the home, isn't an adoptive family pretty much the same as a biological family? The answer is yes and no.

All parents, biological and adoptive, share the same aspirations for their children. We hope to provide them with the best possible beginning, to offer a foundation of love and security, as well as educational and social opportunities. We want to protect them while they are vulnerable, at the same time helping them to achieve their full potential as independent adults. For one child that might mean living in a group home and holding down a job; for another becoming a professional musician or an elementary school teacher. In all cases, the better we do our job, the less, ultimately, our children will need us.

It's the way we must go about achieving these universal goals that distinguishes biological from adoptive families. The two experiences are vastly different. These differences do not disappear once the adoption is complete. Throughout the family life cycle emotional, medical, and social issues arising from the fact of adoption will require attention. Table #1 sets out some of the most important distinctions.

2. Adoption is a world of contradictions

- **Contradiction #1:** "Your mother loved you so much that she gave you up for adoption."

This statement, now out of favor as a way of explaining adoption to a child, summarizes the principal contradiction in adoption. Adoption is built on losses. Birth parents, in losing them, give their children the chance of a better life. Adoptive parents, while gaining a child, lose the opportunity to be that child's biological parents — a loss that applies even to fertile adopters. And adoptees lose their biological roots as

2

TABLE #1
DIFFERENCES BETWEEN BIOLOGICAL AND ADOPTIVE FAMILIES

I. ACCESS TO PARENTHOOD

a. Biological families

- Physically capable couple may reproduce at will.

- Subsequent children may be conceived at option of parents.

- Age is no barrier as long as parents are fertile.

- Unorthodox (i.e., gay, lesbian, single, members of minority, religion) parents may reproduce.

- If in poor health or experiencing disability (e.g., diabetic, obese, wheelchair user, hearing-impaired), parents may still reproduce, if it is physically possible.

- In general, no one is prevented from reproducing because he or she is poor, on welfare, un- or under-employed.

b. Adoptive families

- Opportunity to parent is beyond control of adopters.

- Opportunity to adopt more children is beyond adopter's control; some placements are available only to childless adopters.

- Adopters seen as too young or old or couples with a large gap between their respective ages may have fewer options than more traditionally aged parents.

- Unorthodox adopters may find it difficult to adopt — choices are usually restricted.

- Unwell, obese, or disabled adopters may be barred from adopting, restricted in options, or confined to adopting a child with the same disability.

- All adoptions require cash outlay. Subsidies exist, but coverage for all expenses is rare. Complex legal and agency systems can be intimidating. Assumptions about fitness to parent may favor middle class adopters at the expense of poor adopters.

TABLE #1 — Continued

II. CERTAINTY

a. Biological families

- To achieve conception requires an average of 5 months. Period from conception to birth is almost always 30 to 42 weeks. Parents know how old *they* will be at time of child's entry into the family.

- Timing of subsequent children is within parental control.

- Health insurance generally covers childbirth, pre- and postnatal services. Where birth is not covered by insurance, parents almost always take home a baby. Medical bills may be tax deductible.

- While no one can guarantee a perfect outcome to any parents, a planned pregnancy *usually* results in the birth of a healthy child.

b. Adoptive families

- Timing is beyond parental control. An adoption may take from a few months to eight years or more. Once a child is designated for a family, months or years may pass before that child is placed in the home.

- Timing of subsequent children is beyond control.

- Expenses are seldom known in advance. If adoption fails, fees may not be waived. Insurance against some failed adoptions exists, but costs thousands of dollars. Adoption fees are not tax deductible.

- Of the birth parents who make an adoption plan, about 50% to 66% reconsider and decide to parent the child themselves. Changing laws and policies of other countries may result in abrupt cancellation of adoption programs. A minority of adopters are victims of fraud, paying large fees without receiving a child.

TABLE #1 — Continued

III. ENTITLEMENT

a. Biological families

- Parents have the right to bear and raise a child unless and until proven otherwise.

- Children have sense of entitlement as full members of the family.

- Biological parenting, especially by married couples, is the socially approved "normal" way to parent. A decision to parent is generally not questioned.

b. Adoptive families

- Adopters must demonstrate parental fitness to adoption professionals, birth parents, government agencies, and judges before adoption is granted.

- Children must learn of their adoption, grieve the loss of their biological parents, and adjust to adoptee life.

- Adoptive families are seen as "different." Motives/entitlement to adopt may be questioned. Adopters may experience belittlement of their role as "real" parents, even from family and friends.

IV. PRIVACY

a. Biological families

- A decision to parent may be completely private. If infertility treatment proves necessary, it need only involve medical professionals. Privacy may generally be maintained until pregnancy shows.

- A unicultural, uniracial family is socially "invisible." It will not provoke attention by its very existence.

b. Adoptive families

- Adopters require involvement of and/or permission from social workers, lawyers, police, government agencies, birth parents, and judicial system prior to creation of the adoptive family.

TABLE #1 — Continued

- Multi-ethnic families are highly visible. Strangers will comment on and ask questions about children. Family may be target of overt or covert racism.

V. GENETIC CONTINUITY

a. Biological families

- The biological family ensures genetic "immortality" through conception and birth of children.

- A child may learn of heredity by asking parents and by accessing family medical records.

b. Adoptive families

- The adoptive family has lost genetic continuity, the opportunity to be connected by blood ties to a child.

- Family medical history will not be available if parents are unknown. In closed adoption, to obtain full medical information may require a court order.

VI. CONTROL

a. Biological families

- Parents can prevent endangering the child in utero by avoiding high-risk behavior.

- Legal parenting requires no judicial intervention.

- Parents are authorized to parent a child from birth onward.

b. Adoptive families

- Parents have no ability to protect child in utero or prior to adoption.

- Adoption can only be granted through judicial decree.

- Adopters usually undergo a supervised trial period after child is placed before the adoption is granted.

they acquire a family. Even where all members of the adoption triad — child, birth parents, and adopters — are satisfied that the best decision has been made, that satisfactory outcome is founded on profound loss.

- **Contradiction #2:** Among the children free for adoption, there is 1 healthy Caucasian newborn per 20 would-be adopters, while at the same time thousands of non-white and older children wait for families.

Choice is important in adoption. Children need families who want them, yet most non-relative, would-be adopters are Caucasians seeking white infants, while most of the children free for adoption are non-white and older. These waiting children often have disabilities and special needs.

Many adoption agencies have successfully promoted adoption of children with special needs, but the demand for healthy white babies shows no signs of declining. Competition for them has led agencies to charge enormous fees (above $20,000) for adopting white newborns, while lowering, even waiving, fees for waiting children. Some adoption professionals deplore this development, feeling that it amounts to baby selling on a supply and demand basis and leads agencies to choose the wealthiest rather than the best family for a child. But many agencies defend their approach, as it allows them to offer fuller services to birth parents and to subsidize adoption of hard-to-place children.

Whatever other ethical issues this contradiction raises, the low supply of white babies has led to better services and options for many birth parents. A birth mother who makes an adoption plan carefully can expect payment of her medical and legal bills, possible reimbursement of some living expenses, all or a large say in choosing adoptive parents, and quality counseling before and after adoption. Few of these advantages were available 30 years ago.

Reconciling these contradictions may not ever be possible. But we can be sensitive to the issues they raise and search for a means to address them in our adoptive experience. Adopting a child while supporting efforts to overcome the societal problems that enabled the adoption is one way. Giving attention and respect to differing views is another.

3. Adoption works best when all parties are well-informed

Parties to adoption need to be well informed because most adoption is about choices. A birth mother chooses adoption over the alternative of terminating a pregnancy or parenting the child herself. In today's adoption environment, she plays a major role in selecting the adoptive family. For their part, adopters choose to adopt over continuing infertility treatment, living childfree, or (where possible) parenting biological children. They select the route to adoption and the kind of child they hope to parent.

To feel fully vested in a decision, we need to understand what the alternatives are and be able to make our choice freely. Birth mothers who receive counseling and information about all the alternatives open to them are better positioned to stick with an adoption plan than those who have not had the opportunity to survey their options. Birth mothers who change their adoption plans and adoptive parents who return children to agencies often prove to have been poorly informed when they made their original choices. Adoptive parents who are not informed of risks, stresses, and issues arising from adopting a special needs child may be poorly prepared for parenting such a child.

Adoptees, too, need to be informed. While infant adoptees have no say in their adoption, just as no children anywhere choose their parents, older children are involved in the process and at times have a role in effecting the adoption. The movement to widen access to adoption records reflects the desire of adoptees to reclaim their history. Although progress has been uneven, the trend since the 1960s has been to allow all parties to adoption increasingly more information and options.

4. Adoption services are a consumer issue

The consumer movement has been around for 30 years and yet it seems scarcely to have touched the world of adoption. While the facts that support this assumption are unlikely to be disputed by adoption professionals, it is rare to hear the term "consumer" applied to users of adoption services. Adoption agencies and services are not scrutinized by the consumer groups who regularly rate health insurance providers and nursing homes. And for their part, prospective adopters rarely avail themselves of consumer aids such as the state attorney general, the state adoption specialist, or the Better Business Bureau to seek information or complain about an adoption service. Yet businesses, government agencies, nonprofit corporations, and professionals specializing in adoption are as likely as any others to be of high or low quality, efficient or disorganized, overpriced or a bargain, ethical or unprincipled. There are good adoption services and poor ones. So why isn't adoption seen as a consumer issue? There are four reasons:

(a) We are reluctant to look at the adoption process as a commercial transaction. After all, babies are not consumer goods. But the fact is adoption involves commercial and professional services for which adoptive families pay fees. In fact, many adoption services are supported exclusively by fees paid by prospective adopters.

(b) As adoption specialists Smith and Miroff noted in *You're Our Child* (see the resources at the end of the chapter) adoptive parents experience a lack of entitlement as parents. It is difficult to feel you are entitled to good service when at issue is your very entitlement to any adoption service at all. Fear that adoption agencies and providers will "blacklist" them for complaining about service quality can keep adopters silent in the face of poor or illegal conduct by adoption professionals.

(c) Infertility and its treatment, experienced by many adopters, is disempowering. Being unable to manage what most of the human race takes for granted can lower self-esteem and make people feel their lives are out of their control. Such adopters may approach adoption passively rather than proactively.

(d) The complexity of the adoption process and the many individuals and organizations involved make it hard to know how to hold them accountable. No single entity is charged with policing adoption. Certain adoption services are unregulated in some states, such as facilitators who put parents in touch with international adoption sources. The adoption programs in foreign countries run by regulated domestic adoption agencies are often unregulated, since domestic laws do not apply overseas.

We need to acknowledge that adoption is indeed a consumer issue and that adoption services are as much a product of the marketplace as any others. Scope, price, and quality of service suffer if providers are not held accountable by clients. If no complaints are received about an agency whose fees are 50% higher than the average and business does not suffer, the provider will not lower prices. An agency that promotes adoption of children with special needs, yet offers no post-placement services to adoptive families, is not going to change its practice if families don't object. The lesson of the consumer movement is that when people join together, they can influence corporations, professionals, and even government to provide better goods and services. To do this, we must learn to advocate effectively for our needs.

5. Advocacy is a part of adoption

Advocacy is the art of persuading, and adopters soon learn that this skill is required at every stage of an adoption. When you fill out an agency application, write a letter to a birth mother describing what your family can offer her child. And when you are interviewed by a social worker during your home study make sure you are advocating for your adoption. Even in the most straightforward stepparent adoption, the biological parent must be persuaded to give consent.

Adoption laws worldwide state that the best interests of the child are the paramount consideration in granting or denying an adoption. Thus, your primary advocacy task as an adopter is to persuade the decision-makers — birth parents, social workers, judges — that your adoption is in the child's best interests.

After the adoption is complete, many parents find they must continue to practice advocacy on their child's behalf. Securing special education and medical services, combating racism, and reforming adoption laws are areas in which many adopters have played an advocacy role.

b. WHY DO I NEED TO BE AN ADVOCATE?

As we have seen, only you — the adopter — link every step of the adoption process. You are unlikely to have an advocate whose only allegiance is to you. In most states, for example, adoption attorneys who help arrange independent adoptions have a professional duty to both birth parents and adoptive parents. Their role resembles that of an intermediary or arbitrator, not your exclusive representative or "hired gun." The same applies to independent adoption facilitators. Most agencies view children as their clients, not adopters. This is true regardless of the size of the fee paid by adoptive families. Agencies offer counseling and support services to birth parents as well as adopters. In these situations, agencies will be juggling the needs and desires of three parties. For-profit adoption businesses have proliferated recently. These services, while marketed to adopters, must attract birth mothers to place children with them. To be successful in today's adoption environment, these businesses must serve birth parents along with adopters.

Because adoption involves at least three parties and because the best interests of the child are required to be served by law, no ethical adoption professional can or should address the needs of only one member of the triad. Yet adopters need effective advocacy to make adoptions happen. The answer is that you as a prospective adopter must become your own advocate. The sooner you start, the better your adoption experience will be.

By the time a difficult adoption is concluded, most adopters have acquired impressive advocacy skills. That is one reason why so many go on to start magazines, form support groups, advocate for legislative change, and even start their own services and agencies. You often hear these people say: "If I only knew then, what I know now!" You can and here's how.

c. FOUR STEPS TO BECOMING YOUR OWN ADVOCATE

1. Gather information

Time spent in educating yourself about adoption will more than repay you later. Like choosing a career path or starting a new business, a good adoption requires an investment of your resources. This investment will include expenditures of time and effort as well as money.

Resist the temptation to commit early to a particular adoption path, a common mistake of first-time adopters. Increasingly adopters, like biological parents, are coming to parenthood at an older age. Many have endured years of infertility treatment and the decision to adopt comes with a sense of urgency. Errors made by hurried adopters include

12

signing on with an agency with a dubious track record, trying to adopt from a country that has recently changed its laws to drastically limit international adoption, and working with an illegal "facilitator." These errors can delay or prevent adoptions and may cost thousands of dollars. All can easily be prevented by doing your homework.

2. Explore your options

You've become familiar with the adoption landscape. Now you need to fit yourself into the picture, learn what kinds of adoption are available to you, and explore your feelings about them. What are the advantages and disadvantages of each? Depending on your background, you may find many avenues open to you or that options are more limited. The good news today is that most people can find a path to adoption that works for them. Some will have to try harder, wait a little longer, and be more creative, but with perseverance it will happen.

3. Set your goals

You are now fully committed to becoming an adoptive parent. You know the advantages and drawbacks of the kinds of adoption that are open to you. It's time to choose your path: independent or agency, infant or older child, domestic or international. It also helps to set some process goals at this stage. Most adoptions take at least a year; some take many more. How will you manage to live your life meaningfully while you wait? Setting process goals — how you will stay informed, get support, deal with emotional highs and lows — can help you take charge during a time when it's easy to feel helpless.

4. Create and implement a successful strategy

You know where you want to go; how will you get there? Depending on who you are and what your goal is, this can be simple or complicated. It is also a creative process. Many who were told they couldn't adopt have done so by inventing their own way around the "problem." Wheelchair users have adopted healthy infants, as have families on limited incomes; gay and lesbian individuals and couples have adopted successfully, as have others in their late forties and older. These people all share certain traits: they are well-informed, assertive, flexible, patient, and optimistic.

Finally, for even the best-prepared parent, adoption is not easy. Making your adoption happen may be one of the most challenging tasks you ever face. But you need only look at the radiant faces pictured in an adoption magazine or attend an adoptive parent gathering to see that for the thousands of us who have done so, the joy of parenting our adopted children repays us many times over.

RESOURCE GUIDE

1. Comprehensive sources of information on adoption

- Adoptive Families of America
  3333 Highway 100 North
  Minneapolis, MN 55422
  (612) 535-4829

AFA is the largest adoptive parent organization in the United States. In addition to publishing *Ours*, which contains articles on adoption for and by adoptive families, it holds an annual conference and acts as a clearinghouse for adoptive parenting resources, including adoption-related and multicultural books and toys. AFA operates a 24-hour, 7-day-a-week telephone hot line at the above telephone number. Callers can receive adoption information, support, and referrals.

- National Adoption Information Clearinghouse
  11426 Rockville Pike, Suite 410
  Rockville, MD 20852
  (301) 231-6512

Federally funded, NAIC is a neutral, comprehensive resource on adoption. It offers catalogues, bibliographies, and pamphlets on adoption issues at low or no cost. Video and audio tapes on almost all adoption issues are available and computer searches can be made for specific adoption-related materials.

- North American Council on Adoptable Children
  1821 University Avenue, Suite N-498
  St. Paul, MN 55104
  (612) 644-3036; FAX (612) 644-9848

NACAC holds an annual conference and publishes a quarterly newsletter, *Adoptalk*. Each issue includes a bibliography of adoption materials. NACAC "advocates the right of every child to a permanent, continuous, nurturing and culturally sensitive family, and presses for the legal adoptive placement of any child denied that right."

2. Adoption theory and philosophy

Brodzinsky, David, Marshall Schechter, and Robin Marantz. *Being Adopted: The Lifelong Search for Self.* New York: Doubleday, 1992.

Kirk, H. David. *Adoptive Kinship: A Modern Institution in Need of Reform.* Port Angeles, WA: Ben-Simon Publications, 1985.

_____. *Shared Fate: A Theory and Method of Adoptive Relationships.* Rev. ed. Port Angeles, WA: Ben-Simon Publications, 1984.

David Kirk, in his classic 1964 study of adoptive families, *Shared Fate*, and in later works, examined how adoptive families adapt to their status in our society. A pioneer in the study of adoptive families, Kirk found that some cope with the negatives of being an adoptive family by what he called "rejection of difference," denying that there is any significant difference between theirs and biological families. Many reported that adoption was insignificant to them because they "felt as if they were real parents." These families were likely to deny the losses of infertility and had little empathy with the losses suffered by their children and the birth parents through adoption. Families who adapted by means of what Kirk called "acknowledgment of difference," recognizing that adoption is profoundly unlike biological parenthood, made the best and happiest adjustment to adoption and had better comunication with their children.

Smith, Jerome and Franklin I. Miroff. *You're Our Child: The Adoption Experience.* Rev. ed. Lanham, MD: Madison Books, 1987.

3. General interest adoption periodicals

Any book that discusses adoption law, procedure, specific agencies and sources of children, will be at least partly out of date within a year or two of publication. Adoption periodicals fill gaps by tracking important changes as they occur. They address would-be parents as well as those who have already adopted and will introduce you to the practical realities of adoption. Subscriptions are not expensive. You may also find copies in the libraries of adoptive parent groups (see chapter 3). In addition to *Adoptalk,* try:

- *Adoptnet*
  P.O. Box 50514
  Palo Alto, CA 94303-0514
  (415) 949-4370; FAX (415) 949-5479.

- *Ours*
  (For address, see Adoptive Families of America, above)

- *Roots and Wings*
  P.O. Box 638
  Chester, NJ 07930
  (908) 637-8828; FAX (908) 637-8699
  Articles by adoption professionals and triad members, birth parents, adoptees, and adoptive parents.

- *Reader's Guide to Adoption-Related Literature*
  2300 Ocean Avenue
  Brooklyn, NY 11229
  This annually updated guide tracks books about adoption for all triad members, professionals, and notes adoption publishers and periodicals. It can be ordered free from William L. Gage, editor, at the above address.

TIPS

Whether you're aware of them or not, current professional views on adoption will affect your adoption experience. You can acquire a professional perspective and insight on how adoption professionals view adoptive parents and the issues they consider important by reading articles in professional social work and law journals. (For law journals you may need to seek out a courthouse or law school library.) Most urban public and college libraries subscribe to academic journals. A reference librarian can help you locate them. Look for articles on adoption published over the past few years. Good sources include *Child Welfare, Family Law Quarterly, Journal of Marriage and the Family,* and *Social Work.*

2
GATHERING INFORMATION: THE BIG PICTURE

a. ADOPTION IN NORTH AMERICA

Throughout the world, informal adoption by extended family has been the primary way children come to be raised by people other than their biological parents. While all ancient societies recognized some form of legal adoption, it was a late arrival to the English common law tradition, with the passage of the first adoption law only in the 1850s. The law was needed because the informal system had begun to break down. The industrial revolution and migration to the new world left many children in North America with neither parents nor extended families. While orphan asylums offered a temporary solution, better alternatives were sought. In the mid-nineteenth century, thousands of orphaned children were sent by train from the big eastern cities to farmers in the midwest where they were "put up" in town halls and train platforms to be chosen by families. This practice lead to the term "put up for adoption," still in use today.

Infant mortality was high and babies were rarely sought or available for adoption. But as social attitudes changed, families began to adopt younger children until World War II, when newborns were the most sought after. Early adoption laws didn't mandate confientiality and records were open. But by the 1930s adoption proceedings and records were closed in every state. The recent trend toward open adoption, through which birth and adoptive parents exchange identifying information and maintain contact after adoption, is a major departure after 50 years of secrecy. But, over the thousands of years of adoption history, adoption secrecy has been the exception, not the rule.

While the charge was occasionally heard before, by the mid-1960s it was clear that demand for babies was outstripping supply. White families increasingly adopted minority children, until as a result of objections by groups such as the National Association of Black Social Workers in 1972, this practice was largely restricted. Concerns about adoptions of Native Americans were also raised and a law was passed in 1978 to regulate them. Other social developments operated to reduce the supply of children for adoption.

The end of World War II also heralded a new phenomenon: international adoption. War "orphans," displaced children who were not necessarily orphans at all, were widely adopted. They came mostly from the losing countries: Italy, Germany, Japan, and Greece, and were placed in homes in Britain, France, the former U.S.S.R., United States, and Canada. By the end of the 1940s, the supply of war orphans was exhausted, but the Korean War in the early 1950s opened a new source of children to western countries.

The Vietnam War also saw a brief, intense migration of displaced children to North America for adoption. As with Korea, some were the children of foreign soldiers and local women. Since 1976, when most adoptions from Vietnam ceased, Latin America has become a major source of children for European and North American adopters.

Today, most developed countries have few healthy infants free for adoption, while infertility rates are rising. Canada and Western Europe have fewer available infants than has the United States. Children with special medical and emotional needs as well as sibling groups are waiting to be adopted in all these countries. The United States has seen an enormous increase in children in foster care in the 1980s and 1990s, so that if present trends continue the number could climb to over one million by the turn of the century. Fewer than 10% of these children are available for adoption, however. If one generalization can be made about adoption today, it is that it is in a state of almost constant transformation.

b. A BRIEF OVERVIEW OF ADOPTION LAW

Why do you need to know about adoption law? Won't your agency, lawyer, and/or facilitator take care of all that? The answer is yes and no. Competent adoption professionals know the laws of the jurisdictions they are working in, but even competent professionals can make mistakes. And not every adoption professional is competent. Further, no one has as much at stake as you do in your adoption.

At a minimum, every would-be adoptive parent should know the basic principles of adoption law, the concept of adoption consent, and the procedures for withdrawal of consent in the jurisdiction(s) in which the adoption takes place. Adoption law is not particularly hard to access and understand. Unfortunately, too many adoptions go wrong because a consent was signed too soon or improperly, or adoptive parents didn't understand the limits of their legal rights. Most if not all of these adopters had adoption professionals working with them. Such errors are preventable, but no one is as motivated as you are to prevent them. Make sure you understand what adoption professionals are doing for you, and the laws their actions are based on.

The rest of this chapter focuses on American adoption laws. Canadian readers can turn to chapter 11 for information on how to adopt a child born in the United States or located with the help of a U.S. agency or facilitator. But because American law affects Canadian adopters, it will help you to read the sections below as well.

Many areas of the law are undergoing change, bringing important modifications to adoption procedures. As you work through your adoption, be sure that you and any professionals you work with are up-to-date on these trends, including recent court cases, legislative, regulatory, and policy changes. Suggestions for how to keep abreast of new developments are given in the Resource Guide at the end of this chapter.

1. A working definition of adoption

Adoption is the legal process by which the rights of biological parents to parent their child are voluntarily relinquished by them or otherwise legally terminated, and transferred to an adoptive parent or parents. After the transfer of parenting rights occurs, biological parents are no longer responsible for the support, financial or otherwise, of the child. Adoptive parents assume the same legal rights and responsibilities that biological parents would have had for the adoptee.

2. Areas under state jurisdiction

The power to pass laws governing adoption originates with the states. Each state has its own adoption law which may set out rules for the following:

(a) Who can adopt

(b) Who can be adopted

(c) Who is permitted to arrange or facilitate the adoption

(d) Who must consent to an adoption

(e) What constitutes a valid consent to an adoption

(f) When and how an adoption consent can be revoked

(g) What adoption fees are permissible

(h) Who must be notified of an adoption

(i) Under what circumstances a finalized adoption can be overturned

(j) Confidentiality of adoption records

(k) Circumstances under which access of birth parents and adoptees to adoption records may be permitted

(l) The legal process of adoption

Recent cases well-publicized in the media have made it clear that variations in adoption laws from state to state can lead to serious problems when an adoption is contested. Many state laws are silent on important issues, such as when, if ever, an adoption decree can be overturned. In an effort to bring certainty and uniformity to adoption law in the United States, a model uniform adoption law has been drafted and is currently being reviewed and refined by the National Conference of Commissioners on Uniform State Laws. The ultimate goal is for every state to pass the same law.

3. Areas under federal jurisdiction

Federal laws on adoption take precedence over state laws. Let's assume you are 20 years old and your state adoption law says that anyone who is over the age of 18 may adopt. But the Immigration and Nationality Act says that you must be 25 or older to adopt a child from another country. This means that while you may be able to adopt a child in your own state, you won't be able to adopt a child from outside the country, because the federal law preempts the state law.

The federal government is responsible for immigration and naturalization (becoming a citizen). In addition to issuing passports, the federal government determines who may adopt a foreign-born child and which foreign-born children are eligible for adoption by Americans, as well as the procedural requirements for bringing such children into the country and obtaining citizenship for them.

The federal government has also passed the Indian Child Welfare Act in 1978. This law, described later in this chapter, preempts state laws on adoption of Native American children.

4. Recent federal laws that affect adoption

(a) Adoption reimbursement for adoptive military families

Adoption expenses of up to $2,000 per child up to a ceiling of $5,000 per family per year can be reimbursed to adopters in the U.S. Armed Forces and Coast Guard. Placement, counseling, and legal fees, as well as birth parent medical expenses can be recovered where the adoption is conducted by a non-profit agency. For further details write to the National Military Families Association listed in the Resource Guide.

(b) The Family Leave Act of 1993

Coming into force in mid-1993, the Family Leave Act provides, among other things, that adoptive parents who are federal employees or working for organizations with more than 50 employees, may take up to 12 weeks of unpaid leave per year from their jobs for the purpose of adopting.

5. Areas with shared jurisdiction

(a) Adoption subsidies for children with special needs

In cooperation with state governments, the federal government, through the Adoption Assistance and Child Welfare Act of 1980, makes financial subsidies available to parents adopting special needs children who have been in the care of public agencies. Payments up to the maximum foster parents would receive if the child were in a foster home are available for eligible children up to age 18 or, in some cases, 21. Family income is not a factor in determining eligibility; however it is taken into account in setting the amount of the subsidy.

(b) Interstate Compact on Placement of Children

When you plan to adopt a child who was born and relinquished for adoption in another state, which state's laws apply to your adoption? The answer is both — but they must be coordinated. Each state has signed the Interstate Compact on Placement of Children (ICPC) which sets out rules for inter-state cooperation in matters involving adoption and foster care.

(c) The Hague Convention

It is too soon to say exactly how the Hague Convention on intercountry adoption, described later in this chapter, will affect adoption laws in the U.S. But it is certain that enacting it into legislation will require cooperation between federal and state governments.

c. LEGAL REQUIREMENTS FOR ADOPTION

State and federal laws are passed and amended by state legislatures and Congress. Subsequently they may be reinter-preted or overturned by the courts. Federal courts are also called on to resolve contradictions between state and federal law. Further, if a federal court finds that a state or federal law contravenes the Constitution of the United States, the law will be declared unconstitutional and cease to operate. On that basis a Florida law banning homosexuals from becoming adoptive parents was recently held to be invalid.

1. Domestic adoption of non-relatives within one state

Because of the complexity and changeability of adoption laws, this section sets out minimum basic requirements common to all states. Many states impose additional legal require-ments on top of those listed below. For example, some require that adopters be state residents or prohibit independently arranged adoptions. In the Resource Guide at the end of the chapter, you will be shown how to learn about your own state's laws.

(a) Who can adopt?

Single adults, as well as husbands and wives jointly, can adopt where they are both state residents.

(b) Who may be adopted?

Any child or adult may be adopted who is a legal U.S. resident as well as any internationally born child who is brought into the United States in accordance with federal immigration laws.

(c) Who is permitted to arrange or facilitate the adoption?

Adoptions may be arranged by state-licensed public and private agencies. For adopters who are not relatives or step-parents of the adoptee, a home study is always required prior to the final adoption hearing.

(d) Who must consent to an adoption?

It is important to understand the difference between *consent* and *notice* in adoption. Someone who has the right to consent to an adoption has the power to allow it to go forward or to stop it from taking place. He or she may also have the right to seek custody. If such a person vetoes an adoption, one of two things can happen. A court can decide that the consent can be dispensed with or not. In the latter case, the adoption will be prevented from happening.

A person who has the right to notice of an adoption only, has no power to stop the adoption. That person must be informed, however, within a period of time specified by state law, that an adoption hearing is to be held. That person may also have the right to address the court on the topic of whether he or she thinks the adoption is or is not in the child's best interests. The court can take this opinion into consideration, but is not bound by it.

In every state, the consent of the birth mother is required. Her husband must also consent to the adoption if she was married at the time of the child's conception and birth and/or he meets the state law's definition of "legal father." If the child is in the custody of a legal guardian other than the biological parent(s), that guardian must consent. All states require the consent of the child if the child is over a certain age (in some states as young as 10, in others 14 or older). In cases when the adoptee is a mentally competent adult who consents to the adoption, no other consent is required.

Difficulties arise when the birth mother is unmarried. The birth mother may not know who the father is or prefer not to disclose his whereabouts. Even if he is known, he may be difficult to locate. The law is unsettled in this area, but the trend is for the courts to find that if a birth father is known, diligent efforts must be made to locate him and obtain his consent or have his rights expressly terminated for a valid adoption to take place. Placements, even finalized adoptions, have been overturned and custody returned to biological fathers where courts found their right to consent had been unfairly withheld.

To avoid the possibility of this heartbreaking scenario, I recommend that you make sure the true biological father is located and that he expressly consents to the adoption of his child, even in states which have birth father registries. In an independent adoption it may be wise to seek scientific proof of paternity from the man named as father by the birth mother, so that the wrong man doesn't consent.

Adoption consent may be dispensed with if a court determines that a biological parent has forfeited the right to consent. Where a child has been abandoned, and no attempt has been made to support or communicate with the child, a parent's right to consent may no longer exist. However, because our society upholds the rights of biological parents as fundamental and protected by the Constitution, a court will be reluctant to dispense with a parent's consent without very strong and clear evidence to justify it. Similarly, courts may terminate parental rights of parents whose behavior seriously threatens the child's best interests, as in some cases of abuse and neglect. Here again, courts are reluctant to take this step unless the evidence supporting it is very "clear and convincing." The process of dispensing with consent and terminating parental rights can be a long one, since investigation of the evidence has to be made

25

and a court hearing held on the issue. For adopters, the surest and fastest path to parenthood is to adopt a child for whom all necessary consents are freely and legally given.

(e) What constitutes a valid consent to an adoption?

A birth mother's consent is not valid until after the birth of the child to be adopted. The consent should be in writing. Usually, the birth father and others may give a valid consent prior to the birth of the child.

(f) When and how can a consent be revoked?

Not every state provides for when and how consent can be withdrawn, although most do have such rules. The issue of withdrawal of birth parent consent has been the subject of litigation. Be aware of your state law at the time of your adoption. Even if the law does not expressly provide for when consent may be withdrawn, a recent court decision may affect your adoption. However, if all the needed consents were valid and legally obtained and any time period for consent to be withdrawn has passed, it will be extremely difficult to subsequently overturn the adoption.

(g) What adoption fees are permissible?

Reasonable placement fees charged by licensed agencies and other service providers operating within the law are permissible. While all states forbid trafficking in children, paid adoption fees do not amount to a contract for sale as would the price paid for a car. The fees that adopters pay are fees for adoption services, not for a child. Consequently, if adopters pay a fee to an agency and for some reason the adoption fails, they are not entitled to an automatic refund. Some agencies may provide full or partial refunds under certain circumstances, or provide additional services without extra fees. These refunds are usually for services paid for in advance by adopters but never provided, owing to the failure of the adoption.

Adopters have no legal right to a child because they have paid or are going to pay a fee, no matter how large. However, where fees are paid for services that were never provided, or provided negligently, or in cases of fraud by service providers, adopters may have legal recourse against the agency or facilitator. In such a case, the remedy would be financial compensation, not provision of a child to the adopters. Should an agency, birth parent, or intermediary guarantee you a child in return for a fee, this transaction may amount to "trafficking," an arrangement both unethical and illegal.

(h) Who must be notified of an adoption?

There is no consensus among state laws here. Check your individual state's requirements.

(i) Under what circumstances can a final adoption decree be overturned?

Again, there is no consensus among states; check your particular regulations.

(j) What is subject to confidentiality?

Adoption proceedings are confidential and hearings are closed to the general public. All court records and documents, including the original birth certificate naming the biological parents, are sealed and kept confidential. Limited medical, genetic and social information about biological parents that would not lead to their being identified ("non-identifying information") can be obtained by adopters and adult adoptees in every state.

(k) Under what circumstances is access by birth parents and adoptees to adoption records permitted?

The law is changing rapidly as a result of efforts by birth parents and adoptees to open adoption records. State laws reflect these differences and each state has different rules.

(l) What does the legal process of adoption involve?

Each state's laws set out procedures that must be followed for adoptions in that state. Prior to the final adoption hearing, an investigative home study by someone legally authorized to do it (usually a social worker) must be made of adoptive parents who are unrelated to the adoptee. Each state specifies what information is needed in the report coming out of the investigation.

After the child's birth or when an adoption plan is made, whichever is later, and necessary birth parent consents are given, temporary custody of the child is given to an agency or directly to adoptive parents. Usually when an agency has custody it will then place the child in the adoptive family home prior to finalization. The consents or termination of parental rights must first be found valid before the judge makes an order based on what is in the child's best interests. If the petitioner (the adopters) seeks to dispense with a required consent such as the birth father's, this issue will have to be resolved before the custody order is made.

A document, known as an adoption petition, is submitted along with any substantiating information the state requires, such as written consents and proof that the required parties have been notified. Those entitled to notice of the proceedings must be notified a minimum number of days prior to the date of the hearing so that they can respond to the adoption petition, supporting or objecting to it, if they wish. There may be two hearings, although one or both may be waived in stepparent or relative adoptions. The finalization hearing is held after a post-placement report by an agency or authorized person is made recommending for or against finalization. If a decision is made that a party to the adoption disagrees with, it may be subject to an appeal to a higher court.

2. Domestic adoption of non-relatives involving more than one state

When more than one state is involved in an adoption, the Interstate Compact on Placement of Children (ICPC) applies. If the ICPC rules are not followed, an adoption may not be allowed. Each state and the Virgin Islands subscribes to the Compact. The ICPC also applies to foster care and treatment for juvenile delinquents placed across state lines. Exemptions from the ICPC, discussed in chapters 9 and 10, apply to some relative and stepparent adoptions across state lines.

Each state has a compact administrator, usually an employee of the state agency responsible for adoption and child welfare. When an interstate placement is planned, the compact administrator of the "sending" state (where the birth mother resides and where the child resides or is to be born) sends a form to the administrator of the "receiving" state (where the adopters reside). This form is filled out and returned to the sending state along with information such as the home study and birth parent consents or evidence that parental rights have been terminated. If the information is found satisfactory, the sending state administrator sends a letter to the receiving state administrator saying that the adoption is not considered contrary to the child's best interests. The adoption proceedings can then go ahead in the adopters' home state. Different states interpret the Compact differently. In some, the administrator will not review any paperwork until after the birth of the adoptee. In other states, the process may be started earlier.

The process can be frustratingly slow at times and it is not always clear which state's laws apply. Some adoption attorneys feel that it is best to comply with whichever law is most restrictive. For example, if state A says that no consent can be given by a birth mother to the adoption of her child until 1 week after the birth and state B says that consent may be executed 24 hours after birth, it is best to wait a week even where B is the sending state. In general, adoption proceedings follow the law of the adopters' state.

Operation of the ICPC becomes more problematic in cases where the birth mother temporarily moves to the home state of the adopters to give birth or where adopters move to the birth mother's state for the purpose of the adoption. Such cases are sometimes construed as in-state adoptions. However, courts may be displeased by evidence of "forum shopping" where one party switches residence solely to expedite the adoption. It is best, where more than one state is involved, to obtain sound legal advice.

3. Native American adoption

Historically, Native American children were placed in foster care and adopted out of their communities in high numbers, with little if any regard for preserving their cultural roots. Concern for their future and the future of their communities led to passage of the Indian Child Welfare Act of 1978. This act governs adoption and foster care proceedings in the United States for any child under 18 who is a member of an Indian tribe (including Alaska natives), or who is eligible for membership and the biological child of a tribe member. The law allows for participation by the tribe at any point in the legal proceedings. In an adoptive placement of an Indian child under any state law, before the child can be placed with a non-Indian family, parents must be sought from (in order of preference):

(a) an extended family member of the child, as defined by the child's tribe

(b) an unrelated member of the child's tribe, or

(c) another Indian family.

Individual tribes have authority to modify rules and procedures. Tribes and individual states may make their own procedural agreements as well. Adoption of Indian children is very difficult for non-Indian families. Because some tribes

30

grant membership to people with a small degree of Native American heritage, a child who doesn't appear Native American may come under the jurisdiction of the act. In view of the complexity of the act, be sure to obtain good legal advice if there is even the slightest possibility that it applies. Remember, too, that as an adopter, you may yourself have some degree of Indian heritage. If so, the opportunity to adopt one of the many Native American infants and children who need families may be open to you. See chapter 5 for further information.

4. International adoption

An adult U.S. citizen 25 years or older or a married couple of whom at least one member is a U.S. citizen may adopt an orphan born in another country as set out in the Immigration and Nationality Act. The act defines "orphan" as a child who has no parents owing to their death, disappearance, desertion, abandonment, or separation from/loss of the child. A child with one parent who is unable to care for the child properly can also be defined as an orphan where the parent has legally released the child for emigration and adoption. An orphan petition (form I-600) must be filed before the child's 16th birthday.

To meet these requirements, adopters must usually adopt in the child's birth country first, in accordance with the laws of that country. A few countries permit adopters, in person or by proxy, to acquire temporary guardianship of the child, return to their home country with the child, and complete the adoption there. But most countries prefer to conduct an international adoption according to their own laws before allowing adopters to leave with the child.

(a) Documents required in international adoption

You will need a complete set of documents and forms for each child you are adopting. These forms include the following:

(a) Proof of the adopter(s) citizenship, age, marriage, and prior divorce, if there was one, is required.

31

(b) A home study in which the adopters are favorably recommended as prospective parents, signed by a state-licensed agency. The agency need not be located in the same state where the adopters live, however. If the adopters are residing abroad (as in the case of missionaries or Peace Corps volunteers) a local agent can do the research for the home study which can then be incorporated into the report of a licensed agency in the U.S.

(c) A set of the adopters' fingerprints, which can usually be taken at the adopters' local police station as part of a criminal background check is required.

These documents are submitted to the Immigration and Naturalization Service by the adopters or by their adoption agency along with the I-600A form.

(b) I-600A advance processing of the orphan petition

By collecting the documents listed above and submitting them to the INS along with the I-600A form (available from any INS office), adopters may begin the international adoption process before they have identified the child they are to adopt. Advance processing allows the INS to review the petition and verify that the adopters meet the legal requirements to adopt. The I-600A form is then forwarded to a U.S. consulate or embassy in the child's country at the same time as the prospective adopters are told that their advance processing petition has been approved. This approval is valid for only one year. After 12 months, if no adoption has yet taken place, the process must be repeated.

It is possible to adopt without going through advance processing, but it will take longer since information that has already been processed by the time the adoption takes place with the filing of the I-600A must be assembled and reviewed before permission is given to bring the child into the United States. However, for American families residing out of the

32

United States, simply filing the standard orphan petition, Form I-600, may be possible.

(c) The adoption process

The next step is for the adopters to carry out the adoption in the child's home country, in accordance with the laws of that country. The process is the same for agency and independent adoption.

Adopters assemble a dossier of documents that must be notarized, translated, and authenticated in accordance with the laws of the country where the adoption will take place. Many documents will be the same as those required by the INS. The documents are sent to the child's country and reviewed by authorities responsible for adoption. Before or during this process the adopters receive and accept the referral of a child for adoption.

Through legal proceedings, probably a formal court hearing, the child is adopted (which will almost certainly require the adopters to travel to the child's country on a U.S. passport and a visa issued by the child's country). Or a temporary guardianship order is made allowing the child to be taken to the U.S. for adoption. In guardianship, a proxy such as an agency worker may be permitted to appear in court for adopters who do not travel.

After the adoption, the adoptive parents must obtain a passport for their new child, using the child's new birth certificate naming them as the parents, from the local government. In guardianship, a passport is still required.

An immigrant visa must be obtained for the child from the U.S. embassy or a consulate for which a medical exam conducted by a U.S.-approved physician, proof of the child's orphan status, visa photo, and final adoption decree are needed. If the child is not adopted in the birth country, evidence must be submitted showing that any pre-adoption requirements of the state where the child is to reside have been met. A fee (about $200) must be submitted along with each of the I-600A and I-600 forms.

(d) Readoption in the U.S.

Internationally adopted children should be readopted in the U.S. to make absolutely certain that they are eligible for naturalization as U.S. citizens, since children adopted abroad by U.S. citizens do not automatically become citizens themselves. The readoption process follows the law of the state where the adopters reside. Documents needed include the child's birth certificate, foreign adoption decree, passport, U.S. visa, and "green card." See chapter 8 for further information.

(e) The Hague Convention

The Hague Convention on Intercountry Adoption signed in May, 1993 marks the first attempt to codify international rules on adoption. The convention was drafted by a commission of the Hague Conference on Private International Law, based in the Netherlands. The United States and Canada are permanent conference members. To ensure broad acceptability to countries that both send and receive children for international adoption, the 38 member states were joined by about 30 non-member states in working on the convention. About 60 countries have adopted the final text of the convention and pledged to ratify it, including the U.S. and Canada. If successful, the convention will curb adoption abuses and bring more stability and predictability to international adoption.

The convention's 48 articles set out minimum standards for a valid international adoption. Signatories may be either "sending" or "receiving" countries, or both. For example, the U.S. is a sending country for the purpose of an adoption of a U.S.-born child by a Canadian family, and a receiving country for the purpose of the adoption of a foreign-born child by a U.S. family. In either case, the convention, once enacted into law by each country's government, binds both sending and receiving countries to certain minimum conditions. These countries are free to enact laws which are even more restrictive than those provided for in the convention, but they may not pass laws that permit adoption practices prohibited in the convention.

The preamble states that children have a right to be raised in a loving, understanding family, but if such a family cannot be found within the child's country, intercountry adoption may be in the child's best interests.

The convention will apply to all adoptions of children under 18 between parties to the convention. Before the adoption can take place, the sending country must establish that the adoption is in the child's best interests and that consents have been freely given (the mother's only after the birth of the child). The receiving country must certify that adoptive parents have been found suitable to adopt, have been counseled, and that the child will be eligible for permanent residency there. Direct contact between birth and adoptive parents prior to the adoption is prohibited. Sending countries must preserve information about the child's background, such as family and medical history. And no one is to derive improper financial or other gain from international adoption activities, although reasonable professional fees can be charged and paid.

Each country must certify a "central authority" to oversee adoption proceedings and interact with like authorities of other convention countries. However, central authorities may delegate functions to subcontractors, who are qualified by reason of their ethical standards, training, and experience to carry out those functions. This means that independent international adoption, while subject to government regulation, will likely continue under the convention.

Be aware, when you consider international adoption, that the law will eventually change. But how it changes will not be clear until federal, state, or provincial governments enact the convention. Changes appear unlikely to occur before 1995.

5. Stepparent adoption

About 60% of adoptions are by stepparents. For these, strict procedural requirements may be dispensed with. What makes stepparent adoption unique is that the child is usually living with a biological parent and the prospective adoptive parent. Often the other biological parent has had or maintains some contact with the child. Because of this history, courts are especially likely to require the consent of that biological parent for the adoption. While it is possible to dispense with this consent under certain circumstances (principally where the parent has not attempted to take any responsibility for the child or maintain a relationship), courts will not do so without clear and convincing evidence.

Where the parental rights of the non-custodial parent have been terminated by a court, parental consent is not needed. Where the non-custodial parent consents, the process is likely to be much faster and easier than for non-relative adopters, but where the parent opposes the adoption, it may be far more difficult for the stepparent to adopt successfully. The permission of the stepchild may also be required.

Stepparent adoption can be well worth pursuing, especially where ties with the non-custodial parent are loose or non-existent, because it will give the stepparent legal parental rights should their spouse become incapacitated or die. More on legal requirements for stepparent adoption is found in chapter 9.

6. Relative adoptions

Throughout history, when parents have been unable to care for a child, they have turned to their extended family for help. Even today, when family members may live thousands of miles apart, relatives are often the first choice as adoptive parents. Recognizing the importance of these bonds, many states give judges discretion to waive procedural requirements for relative adopters. The Indian Child Welfare Act expressly gives relatives first preference as adoptive parents.

36

However, it is important to know that if you are seeking to adopt a relative who is a citizen of another country, you must ensure that the child meets the definition of "orphan" in the Immigration and Nationality Act. These requirements are not waived for the child's relatives.

Further discussion of legal requirements for relative adoptions can be found in chapter 10.

d. FOSTER CARE AND ADOPTION

Children who have been removed from their families because of parental abuse, neglect or incapacity, or who are relinquished voluntarily by their parents may be taken into foster care by the state authority responsible for child protection. The children may go to a licensed group home, an institution, or the home of a family licensed by the state to provide foster care. Each state has laws governing foster care within its borders. The Interstate Compact on Placement of Children governs placement of children out of their own states. The Indian Child Welfare Act governs foster placements of Indian children.

Each state sets rules for licensing foster parents. Prospective foster parents are recruited from relatives, through the media, through churches, or among professionals who work with children. If, after screening, applicants are found acceptable, they are usually required to attend parenting classes. This can be essential if the children have special needs. A family of the same racial and cultural background is usually sought for children, but if that's not available, a child may be fostered by a family of another background.

Parents receive fixed monthly payments for each child, in accordance with state law. Medical and other expenses may be covered. If parental rights are terminated, today's foster parents are usually given the first opportunity to adopt the children. However, since many adoption professionals feel children should not be placed transracially, foster parents of another race than their foster child may not be permitted to adopt the child, even if the child has spent years with the foster family. This area is controversial and is the subject of ongoing litigation. For more information on foster parenting, see chapter 5.

e. LEGAL RIGHTS OF BIRTH PARENTS

The right to procreate, to parent a biological child, is protected by the Constitution of the United States. The law assumes that biological parents are capable of being adequate parents until proven otherwise on the basis of very clear evidence. What this means for adopters is that our rights are secondary to those of birth parents until a legally valid adoption has taken place. In the legal adoption process, the Court looks first at the birth parents: have they consented freely to the adoption? Have their rights been properly terminated? Only after receiving an affirmative answer to one of these questions will a judge look at the prospective adoptive parents and consider their petition.

Because our laws protect the rights of biological parents, it is not enough for adopters to prove that we have more to offer a child, that we are likely to do a better job of parenting than the biological parents. You may wonder why the best interests of the child don't require that a judge look at adopters at the same time as the biological parents in coming to a decision. The operating presumption is that living with a biological parent or parents is in a child's best interest. This sometimes seems unfair to adopters, especially where birth parents have at best marginal parenting abilities. But on the other hand, once you are an adoptive parent, you will have the same rights yourself. The presumption that you are fit to parent your child will then be transferred to you.

f. LEGAL RIGHTS OF ADOPTEES AFTER ADOPTION

After a legal adoption has taken place, the adopted child stands in the same position as would a biological child of the adoptive family, with one important exception: the adoptee's birth certificate lists only the adopters as parents. The original birth certificate identifying the birth parents is sealed and kept confidential. The adoptee has no legal right to the original birth certificate or any other identifying information until he or she is an adult. Even then, only three states permit adult adoptees unfettered access to their records. One reason is historical: in the early days of adoption in our legal system, adoptees did not inherit property from their adoptive parents unless they were specifically named as beneficiaries. If their adoptive parents were unable to support them, efforts might be made to seek additional payments from the biological family. Over time the law evolved to the position that adoptive parents have rights and duties identical to those of biological parents. Issuing a new birth certificate means that in the eyes of the law, the adopters are the only legal parents. But while this outcome may resolve issues such as inheritance and child support, it doesn't address the fact that an adoptee actually has two sets of parents.

It is natural for adopted children to wonder about their past and, for some, to seek contact with their birth parents. For many years adopters have been strongly encouraged to share information with their children about their background and the circumstances of the adoption. Unfortunately, in closed or semi-closed adoption, adopters may have little to share. Today, many adoptees are engaged in efforts to open adoption records. Increasing numbers are going back to court to obtain personal information. Children of artificial insemination have also sought, sometimes successfully, the right to obtain information about their parents.

The law is slowly coming to acknowledge the rights of adoptees to learn of their origins in at least some circumstances. At the same time, the rights of birth parents to search for children have gained recognition. In some states, one party to the adoption may hire an intermediary (usually an adoption agency or social worker) to seek out the other party and ask for identifying information. If the party agrees, information may be released. If not, the party seeking it may still petition the court to obtain it. A growing number of states have set up "mutual consent voluntary adoption registries" where a party to the adoption signs up agreeing to release identifying information about himself or herself to another party if requested.

g. LEGAL RIGHTS OF ADOPTIVE PARENTS AFTER ADOPTION

Just how final is an adoption decree? Some states occasionally allow final decrees to be overturned, usually because needed consents were not obtained or were obtained fraudulently. Recently, some adoptive parents have also sought to overturn final decrees years later and return children to the agency that placed them or, if the adoption was independent, to public care. These children were usually adopted as infants on the assumption that they were healthy, but later proved to have serious medical, emotional, or behavioral problems. Children adopted at older ages have also been returned to agencies for the same reason or because the special need causing the disruption was not known at the time of adoption.

Many in the adoption community find this trend disturbing, especially so when it involves children placed as infants. It violates the principle of permanency that adoption is based on and seems to suggest that for some adoptive families, their love and interest in parenting is conditional on their being guaranteed a certain kind of child. The issue is under litigation in several states and far from resolution. A few states recognize the right of adoptive parents to take this action under some circumstances.

Another issue that has arisen as the number of special needs adoptions has grown is the case in which an adoptee proves to have medical, behavioral, or emotional problems not identified at the time of adoption and that require costly intervention. Who should pay for treatment? If the problem was unrecognized before finalization, the family is probably not eligible for state and federal benefits. In these cases, adopters are not seeking to overturn the adoption, but to be compensated for the cost of treatment. Known as wrongful adoption, this issue has been litigated in a number of states and parents have received compensation in some cases where they were able to demonstrate that the placing agency knew or should have known of the problem at the time of adoption and failed to adequately inform the family.

RESOURCE GUIDE

1. History of adoption

Bagnall, Kenneth. *The Little Immigrants: The Orphans Who Came to Canada.* Toronto, Ontario: Macmillan, 1980.

Du Prau, Jeanne. *Adoption.* Englewood Cliffs, NJ: Simon & Schuster, 1990.

Hall, Marilyn Irvin. *The Orphan Trains: Placing Out in America.* Lincoln, NE: University of Nebraska Press, 1992.

Hollinger, Joan et al. *Adoption Law and Practice.* New York: Matthew Bender & Co., 1992.

2. Adoption law

Through the National Adoption Information Clearinghouse (see the Resource Guide at the end of chapter 1 for address) you can order the following:

(a) Copies of federal adoption laws (including the Adoption Assistance and Child Welfare Act and the Indian Child Welfare Act)

(b) *Adoption Laws: Answers to the Most-Asked Questions* (organized by state)

(c) *Matrix of State Laws on Adoption* (organized by issue such as who can adopt, consent, etc.)

For further information on adoption benefits for military families contact:

- National Military Families Association
  600 Stevenson Avenue, Suite 304
  Alexandria, VA 22304
  (703) 823-6632

3. Immigration law

For detailed information on immigration law and procedure in international adoption, write for a free copy of *The Immigration of Adopted and Prospective Adoptive Children* (Form M-249) from:

- U.S. Immigration and Naturalization Service
  Director, Outreach Program
  425 I Street N.W., Room 6230
  Washington, DC 20536

The U.S. State Department is responsible for embassies and consulates abroad. It publishes fact sheets on international adoption by country and offers a telephone adoption hot line with fairly up-to-date information on adopting in Chile, China, Honduras, Peru, Romania, Russia, and other countries. The State Department also employs several adoption specialists whose job is to address specific adopter concerns.

To receive a fact sheet, telephone the number below and/or send a letter with a stamped, self-addressed 9" x 12" envelope to the following address and indicate the country(ies) you are interested in adopting from:

- U.S. Department of State
  Office of Citizen Consular Services, Room 4811
  Washington, DC 20520
  (202) 647-3444

If you have a computer and modem, you can obtain instant access to State Department travel and safety advisories, health alerts, and adoption, immigration, and visa information by calling (202) 647-9225

TIPS

To obtain federal laws and regulations as well as other government publications, contact the nearest U.S. government bookstore. It is usually listed in the phone book. If you live a long way from the nearest bookstore, write for a catalogue of U.S. government publications from —

- Consumer Information Center
  P.O. Box 100
  Pueblo, CO 81002

To keep track of legal amendments, changes of policy, and court decisions for each of the 50 states, there are several excellent resources to tap.

The book Adoption Law and Practice, (see listing above) is a two-volume compendium of state and federal adoption law and legal decisions that is updated throughout the year. Although directed toward attorneys, the book offers an excellent, readable history of U.S. adoption and an analysis of legal issues and interpretation of laws as they change.

It is expensive, but can be found at courthouse and law school libraries as well as some larger adoption agencies and public libraries.

Bar associations offer continuing legal education courses to attorneys to help them keep up with changing areas of practice. Classes are often open to anyone who pays to attend. A half or full day class on adoption law can be expensive, but the fee usually includes written materials and up-to-date information. Since non-specialists often attend these courses, they are pitched to people who don't have a background in adoption practice and much material covered will be general. Call your state bar association to ask how you can get on the mailing list for continuing education classes.

3

GETTING TO KNOW THE PLAYERS

This chapter introduces you to the people and institutions involved in adoption. Knowing in advance who is who and what their role is in the process can help you identify who you need to talk to and whether or not they can help you.

a. PRIMARY PLAYERS

1. Birth parents

The biological parents of a child who has been adopted are known as "birth parents." It is important to understand when and how to use this term. It is applied exclusively to parents who have chosen adoption for their children or whose children have been adopted following termination of parental rights. Some birth parents feel that the term should be reserved for parents who have made a voluntary adoption plan. Parents raising a child born to them are referred to as "biological" parents. In this book I use "birth parents" to refer to any biological parents of children placed for adoption.

I have chosen the term birth parents over birth mothers, in recognition that an increasing number of birth fathers play a role in making adoption plans. However, the fact remains that many birth mothers face the difficult issue of how to plan for their child's future without any support from the father. Sometimes this is the mother's choice and sometimes it is not. It is the mother who carries the child for nine months and who is held most socially responsible for an adoption decision. It is her body that experiences nine months of pregnancy, undergoes labor, and is prepared to nurture the child after birth. From a practical and legal viewpoint we should think in terms of birth parents; from an emotional viewpoint, we need to acknowledge that adoption decisions weigh most heavily on the mother.

2. Birth siblings

Adoptees may have biological siblings who remain with the birth parents or are adopted or fostered by another family. I refer to them as "birth siblings" to distinguish them from biological siblings placed together in a single adoptive family and from families in which children from different biological families are adopted by the same parents.

3. Children free for adoption

These children, also known as "waiting children," have no permanent families. Their biological family ties have been cut, voluntarily or involuntarily, and unless they are adopted, they will remain in legal limbo until they reach adulthood. Today, about 10% of foster children in the United States are free for adoption. By the year 2000, the number may be over 100,000.

Worldwide, statistics are harder to come by. Many children in developing countries retain weak family ties, yet are responsible for themselves from an early age. These children may or may not meet the definition of "free for adoption." In the United States and Canada, such children remain in foster or institutional care until they are adults. Public agencies work hard, often hand in hand with private agencies and adoptive family groups, to find parents for them.

4. Children not yet free for adoption

These are children who may eventually be adopted, but until the issue of parental rights is resolved, they cannot be placed in a permanent family. Meanwhile, they may live in foster homes or institutions. In many informal adoptions where family friends or extended family members assume parental responsibility, the children are not legally free to be adopted and may never be. In other cases, biological parents, while unable to care for their children themselves, fight the termination of their parental rights and the loss of their children in court. In the effort to protect everyone's rights, children are too often the losers, without permanent families or a clear future. Unfortunately, children in this state of limbo form the fastest growing population in adoption.

5. Extended birth family

An adoptee's extended birth family may or may not play a part in the child's life prior or subsequent to adoption. Sometimes a child who is later adopted is first raised by a grandparent, aunt, or older sibling. Depending on their relationship with the child, these extended family members may be deeply affected by the adoption. A child may grieve for a lost grandmother as much as for a parent, which is why open adoptions sometimes provide for ongoing contact with an adoptee's extended family. To maintain such ties can be an enriching experience for everyone. However not every adoption warrants maintaining these connections. In some cases, such as where a child has been subjected to extreme abuse in the birth family, severing ties may be the best alternative.

It is important to understand that extended family members may play a role in the decision of birth parents to place their children for adoption. Where her family opposes the adoption, a birth mother may have difficulty proceeding with an adoption plan. Equally, a birth mother who is pressured into agreeing to an adoption plan by family members, may later regret her decision and decide to parent the child herself after all. Adoption plans seem to work most smoothly where birth parents have the support of their families in making their decision.

6. Foster parents and other temporary caregivers

In international adoption, children sometimes live in foster homes or institutions for years and may form important ties to caregivers. Even if the only contact is with a social worker, it may be well worth maintaining. These people are part of your child's past and identity and can help answer the question we all ask, "where did I come from?"

Prior foster parents and caregivers can also be a good source of information when you are adopting a child with special needs. They can give you the benefit of their experience and offer practical advice, support, and encouragement. Keeping in touch with the people who have cared for your child will almost always be a benefit — to you and your child.

7. Adoptive parents

Adopters come in all shapes, sizes, ages, sexual orientation, religions, races, cultures, educational levels, incomes, and professions. Adopters are victims of stereotyping, especially stepmothers who are depicted as evil in almost every fairy tale. Some (including, all too often, health care, education, and social work professionals) see adopters as responsible for any problems their children may have or develop. Others see us as guardian angels — adopting out of the goodness of our hearts to "rescue" needy children, instead of being motivated by the simple desire to be parents like any others.

Adoptive parents, out of necessity, learn a hard truth — that as much as we'd like to think otherwise, our children are not simply extensions of ourselves. They are free human beings in their own right. We also know that you don't have to be genetically, culturally, or racially related to children to love them. In our troubled, deeply divided world, that is a truth worth knowing.

8. Adoptive family siblings

(a) Biological children

Adoptive families often include biological as well as adopted children. Adopters may go on to give birth to biological children after adopting, sometimes with the help of new infertility treatments. Secondary infertility and other health problems lead families to adopt after having biological children. In stepfamilies, biological and adopted siblings may grow up together, and most preferential adopters adopt before and/or after having biological children.

Despite these facts, when we talk about the "adoption triad," we often forget to include biological children of adoptive parents. These children have adoption thrust upon them. While parents may wish to provide a sibling for their child, they don't ask the child's permission to do so. Instead the child suddenly acquires a sibling and in addition to the usual adjustments a child must make when a sibling arrives, must make even more. Children see their parents worrying about whether an adoption will happen. In the worst scenario, a baby may be placed in an adoptive home for months or longer, only to be abruptly removed when a court orders the return of the child. In our case, we received two referrals of baby girls from Brazil whose mothers later decided against adoption. Our lawyer had sent us wonderful photos that we shared with our four-year-old son, so he was confused and upset when we had to tell him not once but twice that the baby pictured in a photo was not going to be his sister after all. Chapter 12 discusses how and when to involve your child in the adoption process.

(b) Other adoptive siblings

Adoptive siblings who are unrelated biologically may come from very different backgrounds. Owing to rapid changes within the adoption system, a child who was adopted in a closed process may have a younger sibling whose adoption is open and where ties with the biological family are sustained. It is natural for adoptive siblings from different birth families to compare their background and experience. Adopters need to be sensitive to the variations in their children's pasts and to find something unique and positive in the background of each child.

9. Extended adoptive family

Adoption changes a family tree. All your relatives, however remote, will be affected by it. Go back and look at Table #1 and ask yourself which of those issues will affect your own family. If you are adopting out of infertility, look at the chart of infertility and adoption losses in chapter 4. Some of those will affect your extended family as well.

Your parents may be especially affected. Their losses are twofold: they are saddened by your losses because you are their child and they have lost the chance to be biological grandparents of your child or, at any rate, of the child you are adopting. Where the adoption is of a child other than a healthy newborn of your own race, it may be more difficult to convey why you have made this choice.

Some extended family members have prejudices against adoption, period. These people will ultimately be your child's family and it is worthwhile to make the effort to introduce them to the idea of your adoption in as positive a way as possible. Chapter 12 offers suggestions for when and how to discuss your adoption with your family.

b. SECONDARY PLAYERS: AGENCIES AND ORGANIZATIONS

1. Public adoption agencies

A public adoption agency, usually located in the department of state government responsible for child welfare, oversees the adoption of children in public care. Commonly, these children have been removed from their biological parents or voluntarily relinquished by them to the custody of a child welfare authority and placed in foster or group homes. Children whose birth parents' rights have been terminated or are in the process of termination may be adopted directly from these agencies. These are usually the least expensive adoptions available. Public agencies may also cooperate with private non-profit agencies to find foster and adoptive families for these children.

2. Private non-profit adoption agencies

Once the primary route for the adoption of healthy Caucasian newborns, private agencies now place more older and minority children and facilitate more international than domestic infant adoptions. Most agencies will gladly place healthy newborns when they have the chance. Often, because they have many potential parents for them, agencies are very selective about who they will allow to adopt healthy infants.

These agencies are incorporated as non-profit corporations. Their income is derived from fees paid by adopters, tax-deductible contributions, and grants from government, foundations, and corporations. They are licensed by state authorities. In the past, agencies always became legal guardians of children placed for adoption by birth parents. Today, agencies may not acquire legal guardianship of infants they place in adoptive homes; instead they may act as facilitators, bringing birth parents and adopters together, arranging for services for each, from counseling to legal advice.

3. For-profit adoption agencies

This small but growing sector of adoption service providers is made up of for-profit businesses, analogous to law firms or medical practices. Their income is generated by adopter fees. They often specialize in providing healthy Caucasian infants to infertile couples and fees are usually high. To place children, these agencies must be licensed by their state, like non-profit agencies. Some have experienced serious financial problems, while others have flourished. Many also engage in international adoptions.

4. Government agencies

The INS and State Department were discussed in chapter 2. The other federal agency involved in adoption is the U.S. Department of Health and Human Services (HHS), Administration on Children and Families. HHS administers adoption subsidies under the Title IV-E adoption assistance program.

In addition to placements by public agencies described above, state agencies administer federal adoption subsidies under Title IV-E and their own adoption subsidy programs for children not covered by Title IV-E. These usually include medical and maintenance payments and special services. Adoption costs may be covered such as court and lawyers' fees. Unlike the federal government, each state sets different standards for eligibility. Some states may apply a means test to determine eligibility.

Local governments also get involved. As part of the home study process, a background check is usually made of adoptive parents by the local police authority of the city or county in which the adopters reside. It includes a search of state records to learn if the adopters have criminal records and/or outstanding arrest warrants.

Every adoption requires adopters to produce certified copies of important documents. Birth certificates, marriage certificates, divorce certificates and death certificates may all be required. Court certified copies can be ordered from the local or state government vital statistics or records department located where the birth, marriage or divorce occurred.

5. Notaries

Notaries are individuals licensed by the state to witness signatures and, where relevant, to hear an oath that the contents of a document are the truth. Documents that haven't been court certified, such as reference letters, home studies, medical and police reports usually must be notarized. A small fee may be charged. Notaries may be public officials. Hospitals, banks, real estate, and law offices also have notaries. Where there are many documents to notarize, it is worth looking for a notary who will waive fees. Banks or doctors' offices may be willing to notarize documents for free.

In international adoption, notarizations require a further step — verification by the local and/or state government. The government agency responsible for licensing notaries verifies that the notarization is valid and attaches a document saying this to the notarized document. The verification requires the verifier's signature. A fee is charged for each verification. Procedures vary by state.

6. Adoption exchanges

Nearly all states have some form of publicly funded adoption exchange. These spin-offs from public adoption agencies work to promote adoption of children who are in public care and are ready to be adopted.

Exchanges often work with private agencies. They provide photos and information about waiting children to agencies and parent groups for circulation. National and regional exchanges help match children and families from across the country. Many newspapers and some TV stations have a daily or weekly feature, often called "Today's Child," that describes a waiting child and the kind of family the exchange feels would best meet the child's needs. In addition, when adopters seek a child through a public agency, they may be referred to the exchange after their home study has been completed. The exchange will then go through all their listings and work on creating a good match of adopters and child. Exchanges concentrate their efforts on the hardest to place children.

7. Facilitation services

Many states have services that stop short of actually placing children for adoption, but which provide information and tools to help independent adopters. Some of these services may be licensed, but many are not. As with agencies, the range in quality is great.

Helping adopters plan and carry out an independent adoption at home or internationally are the two most common services provided. A facilitation service might help prospective adopters prepare a description of their family, place an advertisement seeking a birth mother in the newspaper, negotiate with birth parents, and make referrals to social workers, lawyers, medical, or counseling services.

8. Courts with jurisdiction over adoption

State courts have jurisdiction over adoption. Which one is used usually depends on where the adopters live. When a child is adopted in accordance with the Interstate Compact, the adopters' place of residence, not the child's birthplace, determines which court hears the adoption petition. Children adopted abroad are readopted in a court determined by the adopters' place of residence. To unseal adoption records requires an application to the court which heard the original adoption petition.

Courts, especially those in urban areas, can be a good resource. Those readopting without an attorney or who need answers to procedural questions, can usually get them answered promptly and accurately by calling the court clerk's office.

c. SECONDARY PLAYERS: INDIVIDUALS

1. State-employed adoption social workers

Social workers license and place children with foster parents, decide when to remove a child from biological parents, and track the family through placement. Biological parents are offered support and services that may help them to parent successfully. If that is not possible, social workers may recommend termination of birth parent rights or adoption of a child by the foster family, or work with an adoption exchange to facilitate a match between prospective adopters and a waiting child. They may also assist adopters in applying for federal and state adoption subsidies.

2. Guardian ad litem

A guardian ad litem, also known as a court-appointed special advocate, is often a trained volunteer appointed by the court to represent the interests of minors or adults who are not mentally competent. If birth parents are under legal age in their state, a guardian ad litem may be appointed to represent their interests in the adoption proceedings. In some adoptions involving older children, a guardian ad litem may also be appointed.

3. Staff of adoption agencies and facilitation services

Some agencies employ only staff with degrees in social work, while others hire workers with different backgrounds. Some have no education and little training in adoption issues. Others have no educational background in social work, but bring a wealth of relevant personal and work experience to the job.

What applies to licensed service providers is even more true for unlicensed facilitators. No authority is charged with the task of making sure an unlicensed service provider is qualified. Unlicensed facilitators may be newly adoptive parents with little breadth of adoption experience however well-intentioned.

4. Doctors

Doctors used to play a significant role in bringing adopters and birth parents together. An unmarried woman would seek help from her physician in making an adoption plan and from among his or her patients or those of a colleague, the doctor would find suitable parents. Although less common today, this still occurs occasionally in independent adoptions. Prospective adopters are often encouraged to send a photo and description of their family to gynecologists, obstetricians, and family physicians across the country, asking the doctor to bring them to the attention of pregnant patients considering adoption. Adopters then come to an arrangement with birth parents directly or through another intermediary, such as a lawyer or facilitator. In considering this approach, be aware that doctors may receive hundreds of these requests every year.

5. Adoption attorneys

Attorneys play many roles in independent adoptions, from seeking and locating birth parents to representing adopters in preparing and submitting an adoption petition. Agencies contract with lawyers to prepare the legal paperwork and to represent the adopters and agency in court. Some adoptions may not require a lawyer, but often, as when contracting with birth parents in an independent open adoption, retaining one is indispensable.

Attorneys facilitating open adoptions usually represent the adopters who pay their fees, not birth parents. However, lawyers also have a professional duty to ensure that birth parents without their own lawyers are fully aware of their rights. In some states, the law requires that adopters and birth parents be represented by different lawyers.

6. Adoption counselors

The complexity of modern infertility and adoption issues has led to a proliferation of counselors who specialize in adoption. Services offered include decision-making and grief counseling for infertile adopters, birth parent decision-making and grief counseling, family counseling for adoptive families, specialized counseling services for adoptive children with special needs (such as a prior history of abuse), and search and reunion counseling for all members of the adoption triad. Many work in private practice; some are employed by adoption agencies. Adoptive parent support groups, search and reunion groups, adoption attorneys, and agencies can usually provide referrals to adoption counselors.

d. ADDITIONAL SECONDARY PLAYERS IN INTERNATIONAL ADOPTION

1. Foreign courts

In most international adoptions today, the adoption is finalized by a court in the country of the child's birth. In some countries, adoption laws vary province by province; in others, a federal law governs all adoptions. Most likely, the court that has jurisdiction over an adoption will be located in the town or region of the child's birth and/or birth mother's residence.

Adopters may find that one person's experience may be utterly different from that of someone who adopted a year before or later. China, Romania, and Brazil, among other countries, have enacted new adoption laws since 1990. To add more confusion, countries which have signed the Hague Convention will all amend their laws on adoption to conform to the new accord.

2. Translators and interpreters

In an international adoption, your dossier must be translated into the language of the country (or region, if more than one language is used there) before the adoption can be processed. Translation is done either in the adopters' or the child's country. Some countries have rules about who is authorized to translate official documents. For those who travel to adopt, an interpreter will probably be needed, at the very least for the court hearing and any other official encounter, such as obtaining the child's passport. For information on how to find translators and interpreters, refer to chapter 12.

3. Out-of-country adoption agencies

Some countries, including Korea and Colombia, require that international adoptions be carried out under the auspices of government-run or authorized adoption agencies. There, adoption procedures are generally simpler, more predictable, faster, and cheaper than in other countries. We will probably see more of these after the Hague Convention is enacted, since each country is required to process international adoptions through a central authority.

4. Orphanages

Every country has orphanages. As in North America, many house children who are not orphans, but whose parents are unable to raise them. Some are run by governments, others by churches and aid organizations. These are often over-crowded and while every effort is made to meet emotional as well as physical and educational needs of the children, few have adequate staffs to accomplish this properly. Most of these children suffer enormous deprivation. It is important, whether adopting through an agency or independently, to learn as much as possible about a child's history of institutionalization before making an adoption decision.

5. Adoption facilitators

There are many kinds of facilitators operating in international adoption today and the difficulty of regulating them was one concern addressed by the Hague Convention. It appears that all facilitators in countries adopting the Hague Convention will eventually be regulated.

Some facilitators are based in the adopters' country and use their personal international adoption experience or a connection with a particular country to help adopters find a child, and prepare for and get through the adoption in the child's country. Some are naturalized U.S. citizens, familiar with the laws and language of the country.

Facilitators also work out of the sending country, often through a U.S. intermediary, and shepherd adopters through the process. The best are usually attorneys or social workers, discussed below. They offer services analogous to U.S. facilitation services. There are, however, some entrepreneurs who "find" children for adoption. In the worst cases, they may be involved in baby snatching, buying children from birth families, and bribing government officials. Chapter 8 discusses how to evaluate facilitators.

6. Social workers

Adoption social workers in many countries work with or are employed by the court system. Where it is legal, they may make referrals of children for adoption.

7. Attorneys

Many developing countries have attorneys who specialize in international adoption. Not all operate legally. Foreigners are often willing to pay fees several times the average annual income and many do not bother to verify that their lawyer is operating within the law. The temptation to make many placements and win high fees has led some lawyers to engage in illegal and unethical practices. Sometimes, families in the child's country are told no children are available for adoption by attorneys who in fact are placing children with European or North American families. The attorneys know that no local family could afford the high fees they can command from adopters in more affluent countries. Babies have also been kidnapped and sold to foreign adopters, sometimes involving collusion of doctors, lawyers, and adopters.

8. Embassies and consulates

All countries with which we have diplomatic ties have an embassy to represent them in Washington, D.C. or Ottawa. Many also have consulates in large cities that deal with trade matters and issue visas to travelers to their country in accordance with their country's laws. Countries issue different visas for different travel purposes. An embassy or consulate must usually review and authenticate an adoption dossier before it is sent to the child's country. Procedures and rules vary by country. Usually, the consulate closest to the adopters' place of residence has jurisdiction. Embassies and larger consulates may have staff familiar with adoption who may be able to provide information to prospective adopters, if the country engages in a high volume of international adoption.

Just as foreign embassies represent their countries here, ours represent us abroad. However, they have no jurisdiction whatsoever over adoptions conducted in accordance with the laws of the child's birth country. In fact, they are likely to be unsympathetic to Americans who have been involved in unethical or illegal adoptions, wittingly or unwittingly. But if an American citizen gets into trouble in the country, they may be able to offer some assistance, short of intervening in the country's domestic affairs.

U.S. embassy and consular personnel have the power to grant visas to foreigners seeking to enter the United States, including children adopted by or under guardianship of U.S. citizens. Embassy and consular staff will make every effort to verify that an adoption order conforms to the country's laws before issuing a visa to the child. They can be expected to be familiar with the country's adoption laws and, in cases of irregularity, may refuse to issue a visa until the matter is resolved.

Americans have occasionally adopted in countries which have no diplomatic relations with the U.S. In such cases, the nearest U.S. embassy located in a third country that has ties with both countries is usually the one which will issue a visa for the child. Such adoptions can be extremely risky and are not recommended.

e. TERTIARY PLAYERS

Addresses are given for many of these organizations in the Resource Guide.

1. International children's aid organizations

Many organizations exist whose mission is to support the rights of children worldwide to food, health, education, and opportunity. The United Nations organization, UNICEF, and Defense for Children International are two. Organizations promoting health, and providing famine and disaster relief include OXFAM, CARE, and the International Red Cross. Many churches operate international aid efforts. While these agencies do not facilitate adoption, many adoptive families join their efforts as volunteers.

2. National organizations for child protection

The Child Welfare League of America (CWLA) advocates for children and publishes a wide range of materials on children's issues. CWLA members include social workers and other professionals and volunteers who work with children. The North American Council on Adoptable Children and the Children's Defense Fund advocate for children's rights. The National Foster Parents Association supports foster families.

3. National organizations for adoptive families

Several organizations represent adoptive parents of every kind at the national level. Adoptive Families of America (formerly OURS) is one. The National Adoption Center provides information and helps match waiting children with families across the U.S. The National Council for Adoption (NCA) produces periodic fact books assembling statistics on adoption, one of the few such resources available. NCA supports preservation of confidential adoptive placements.

4. Adoption information clearinghouses

The National Adoption Information Clearinghouse is a publicly funded resource for every kind of adoption issue. In international adoption, the International Committee for Children's Concerns (ICCC) is a good resource. Unlike NAIC, ICCC is a private, non-profit organization. It publishes an annual adoption guidebook, which, in addition to general articles, lists U.S. adoption agency programs for each country which allows international adoption.

The ICCC also publishes a catalogue of waiting children that is updated frequently, offers photos and brief descriptions of children waiting for families, and tells how to enquire about them. The ICCC has a computer database on international adoption and will conduct a search on request for a small fee.

5. State adoption councils and local adoption services

Several states have adoption councils which are organizations concerned with adoption issues. They act as state-wide information clearinghouses on adoption. Some cities or regions have also funded organizations to provide adoption information to the public or provide adoption-related services. They are usually listed in the phone book.

6. Adoptive parent support groups

Hundreds of these grass-roots organizations thrive throughout North America. A large city may have many groups representing different parent constituencies; other groups represent any adoptive parents within a geographic area. Most produce newsletters and many list waiting children available through agency programs or adoption exchanges. They sponsor play groups, waiting parent support groups, summer camps, and cultural celebrations. Many are well respected in their communities and work with public and private agencies to promote high quality service, and many address adoption issues. Some have lending libraries of materials on adoption. Inquiries from prospective adopters are encouraged and they put them in touch with needed resources. Some larger adoption agencies sponsor support groups for parents who have adopted or who are planning to adopt through their agency.

Recognition that the emotional consequences of adoption can last a lifetime has led to the development of birth relative and adoptee support groups. Some exist to help birth parents considering adoption and offer support in living with it afterward. A few have taken strong positions against adoption, advocating instead for stronger birth parent support services and, where necessary, a form of guardianship which does not sever legal ties between birth family members.

Through adoptive parent groups, some child welfare organizations, and adoption agencies, support groups for adoptees have grown up. Groups are provided for children, teenagers, and adult adoptees. The focus is usually on dealing with adoption issues as they relate to the rest of the adoptee's life.

Some birth parents and adoptees feel a strong need to search and find each other. Search and reunion groups also

61

exist in every state to support members through the decision to search, offer help in going about it, and help in dealing with the consequences once a family member has been found. Advice on how to search and referrals to search consultants and counselors is offered. Many engage in lobbying state and federal governments to open adoption records. Adoptive parents are well represented in these groups. For further information see the chapter 14 Resource Guide.

f. ILLEGAL ADOPTION AND FRAUD

There has always been a black market in adoption. Working with an adoption agency is no guarantee against an illegal adoption, especially agencies that facilitate international adoptions, since they may rely on the word of intermediaries they know little about. Who are the black marketers? They are often entrepreneurs, preying on an easy target — adopters who desperately crave parenthood and are too naive or obsessed to take the time to verify that their adoption is legal.

As adoptive parents, you will one day have to explain to your child how he or she was placed for adoption. I believe that you owe it to your child to be able to say that it was done within the law and with the child's best interests in mind by all parties involved. If you bribed a judge, paid cash to an intermediary who promised that "everything would be taken care of" without first learning what that meant, if you simply took the word of one person that your adoption was legal without separately verifying that it was, you will one day have to tell your child this story and either lie about the circumstances of the adoption or let your child know that you tolerated a process that may have been illegal or unethical.

So many black market adoptions occur each year, domestically and internationally, that if you don't work to make yours legal, it could prove to be one of them. And finally, if you are discovered in the process of carrying out an illegal adoption, you may be dooming yourselves to remain childless. Suggestions for evaluating agencies and facilitators which can reduce the chance of illegality in your adoption are found in chapters 7 and 8.

RESOURCE GUIDE

1. Books about how adoption affects families

Arms, Suzanne. *Adoption: A Handful of Hope*. Berkeley, CA: Celestial Arts, 1990.

Johnston, Patricia Irwin. *Perspectives on a Grafted Tree*. Fort Wayne, IN: Perspectives Press, 1983.

Silber, Kathleen and Phylis Speedlin. *Dear Birth Mother*. San Antonio, TX: Corona Publishing Co., 1982.

Sorosky, Arthur D., Annette Baran, and Reuben Pannor. *The Adoption Triangle*. Garden City, NY: Anchor Books, 1979.

2. International organizations that work with and advocate for children

- Defense for Children International
  21 S. 13th Street
  Philadelphia, PA 19107
  (215) 569-8850

- Joint Council for International Children's Service
  from North America (JCICS)
  2372 – 18th Street
  San Pablo, CA 94806-3504
  (415) 486-4583

- OXFAM America
  115 Broadway
  Boston, MA 02116
  (617) 482-1211

- The United Nations Children's Fund (UNICEF)
  3 UN Plaza
  New York, NY 10017

- U.S. Committee for UNICEF
  331 E. 38th Street
  New York, NY 10016

3. National organizations that work with and advocate for children

- Child Welfare League of America
  440 First Street N.W.
  Suite 310
  Washington, DC 20001-2085
  (908) 225-1900

- Children's Defense Fund
  P.O. Box 7584
  Washington, DC 20077-1245
  (202) 628-8787

- National Foster Parents Association
  Information and Services
  226 Kilts Drive
  Houston, TX 77024-6214
  (713) 467-1850

4. National adoption organizations

- (AFA and NACAC listed in chapter 1 Resource Guide)

- National Adoption Center
  1500 Walnut Street, Suite 701
  Philadelphia, PA 19102
  1-800 TO-ADOPT

- National Council for Adoption
  1930 Seventeenth Street N.W.
  Washington, DC 20009
  (202) 328-1200

5. Clearinghouses

- International Concerns Committee for Children
  911 Cypress Drive
  Boulder, CO 80303
  (303) 494-8333

- (NAIC listed in chapter 1 Resource Guide)

6. Adoptive parent support groups

There are several excellent guides that list adoptive support groups in the United States and Canada. NAIC publishes the National Adoption Directory. For each state it lists public and private adoption agencies, adoption exchanges, attorney referral services, parent support groups, post-adoption services, adopted person and birth relative support groups, as well as the state licensing authority. The guidebook costs about $25. *Ours* magazine publishes frequently updated lists of adoptive parent support groups by state.

TIPS

It's easy to see that avoiding a black market internationaal adoption is important, but how do you do it? The first step is to inform yourself on what constitutes a legal adoption in the country involved. The U.S. State Department (address at the end of chapter 2) is a good place to begin. Call the telephone line, send for fact sheets and, if the country you are considering isn't included, write or call and ask to speak with someone responsible for helping adoptive families. You might also contact the country's embassy in Washington and ask for information.

Consider subscribing to *Adoption Helper*, listed in the chapter 11 Resource Guide. While the publication is Canadian, each issue includes a country-by-country update of international adoption laws and practices. Call the AFA HELP line and the NAIC. Both respond to telephone queries about adoption. The Joint Council for International Children's Services (JCICS) from North America may also be able to give you information. Larger, reputable adoption agencies (Children's Hope, Holt, and WACAP are good examples) will be familiar with the adoption law of countries they place from. See chapter 7 for information on contacting agencies.

If you are unable to get consistent, satisfactory information about a country's adoption laws after trying these options, you should reconsider your plans. Lack of clear, accessible legal guidelines for international adoption is a sign of trouble. There are plenty of other countries to adopt from whose adoption laws are easy to access and understand.

4
EXPLORING YOUR OPTIONS: READINESS FOR ADOPTION

a. THE SHIFTING INTERFACE BETWEEN INFERTILITY AND ADOPTION

For those experiencing disability or infertility, there has never been a better or a worse time to be infertile. In recent years, new drug therapies and alternative reproductive technologies have offered hope for the first time to many seeking parenthood. Fifty percent of those undergoing treatment for infertility will eventually be successful. For those who can be easily helped by these new therapies and who are fortunate enough to have adequate health insurance and/or sufficient funds to expend on treatment, the picture is a rosy one. But for those whose prognosis is uncertain, whose resources are limited, or who take advantage of new treatment options to no avail, the outlook is bleaker. And for everyone struggling to deal with infertility, the journey from treatment to resolution has never been more complicated than it is today. To make this transition successfully, it is important to understand how the boundaries between infertility and adoption are shifting and what that means for those who must decide between continued pursuit of fertility, living childfree, or adopting.

1. More diagnosis and treatment options for infertility

Until recently, diagnosing infertility with certainty was difficult and most forms were, in any event, untreatable. Today, all that has changed. A couple having failed to conceive after 18 months is referred by their primary physician to an infertility clinic where specialists conduct an extensive evaluation. In addition to blood work and semen analysis, diagnostic procedures might include ultrasonography and microsurgery. The cost of diagnosis alone is measured in thousands of dollars and months of physically taxing procedures.

If the couple is lucky enough to receive a clear diagnosis, treatment options are almost always multiple. Many begin with drug therapies which require at least six months for a reasonable trial. Should these prove unsuccessful, the couple must decide whether to undergo ever more expensive and invasive procedures, with an ever declining likelihood of success. The more they invest unsuccessfully in their search for infertility, the harder it becomes to end treatment, even after it has failed. It is, after all, difficult to give up on something to which we have devoted years of our lives and on which we have spent our life's savings. And yet, despite the high cost, each year more than one million patients seek medical help for infertility.

It is common to find couples who have spent ten years or more in active unsuccessful infertility treatment. Deciding to move from treatment to adoption has never been more difficult, while the stakes are higher than ever before.

2. Prospective parents are older

More and more people are seeking parenthood in their mid-to late thirties and beyond. Infertility specialists report that the past decade has seen a huge increase in the number of would-be mothers over 40. Since fertility declines with age, the prospects for biological parenthood for many are poor to non-existent. Yet, because many adoption avenues are also restricted to those over 35 or 40, there is small incentive for infertility patients to switch to adoption.

The longer an older couple spends in infertility treatment, the poorer the prognosis and the more they may foreclose their adoption options. Thus it can be hard for the older couple to make a decision to move out of infertility treatment into adoption. But, as we'll see in chapter 5, there are more options available for older adopters than are popularly believed. For many over 40, adoption will provide a faster, less expensive route to parenthood than continued treatment for infertility.

3. Adoption is more complicated today

The infertile married couple of the 1950s had a simple path to adoption and few decisions to make along the way. Private adoption agencies were few and international adoption was rare. Open adoption was unheard of and birth records were seldom unsealed. There were usually more healthy newborn babies available than families to adopt them. Today's infertile married couple has both more options and more hurdles to negotiate. The non-traditional family had few if any options 40 years ago; now the picture is brighter for every kind of person who was earlier excluded from adoptive parenting.

Today adoption is dauntingly complex. Many of the players on the adoption scene described in chapter 3 didn't exist 30 years ago; there may be as many as ten times the number of adoption agencies in existence now. Adoption litigation has become more common and news stories of adoption gone wrong appear frequently. Moving from infertility treatment with its limited cast of players to adoption with its cast of thousands can be intimidating.

b. LOSS AND GRIEVING IN INFERTILITY VERSUS ADOPTION

As we have seen, making the decision to move from infertility treatment to adoption is harder than ever before. At this stage, neither alternative is a sure thing. But for many who are infertile, adoption offers a more realizable path to parenthood than does further treatment. Yet even when it is possible to say objectively that the odds of success are better in adoption than in infertility treatment, how do you know adoption is the best choice for *you*? And how can you tell that you are emotionally ready to take this step?

Professionals agree that there is no litmus test for adoption readiness, but certain pointers do exist. Excercise #1 and Table #2 contrasts losses arising from infertility with losses from adoption. As the list indicates, some losses experienced by infertile people are lifelong, persisting even into adoption. There are some in the adoption community who believe that these losses must be fully resolved prior to adopting. More recently, though, many professionals have concluded that dealing with loss is not a simple, linear process. They believe that our experiences of fundamental loss ebb and flow over a lifetime. However, acknowledging the impact they make on us emotionally whenever these feelings arise, grieving irrecoverable losses and formulating a strategy for dealing with them are necessary steps to making the successful transition to adoption.

The process of acknowledging losses includes grieving them. You have lost the biological child you and your partner might have created together and it is necessary to mourn this loss, just as you would mourn the death of a child born to you. This is not a linear process. As with other kinds of mourning, time will relieve the pain, but certain events may activate it again. The joyful arrival of a long-awaited child of adoption may provoke a sharp sense of loss of the unborn biological child.

The importance of coming to terms with the grief of infertility to the greatest extent possible cannot be overemphasized. Those who rush into adoption consumed by the frustrations of infertility and anger at the barriers standing between them and their goal of a child are vulnerable to making poor adoption choices. These include making hasty decisions on what kind of child to adopt and from what source, entering into a dubious independent adoption agreement with the likelihood of failure, and engaging in black market/illegal adoption either domestically or in a foreign country. Poor choices are responsible for many failed adoptions and even if the adoption is

EXERCISE #1
ADOPTION READINESS

The exercise:
The first step in readiness decision-making, is to weigh the relative importance of infertility and adoption losses in your life. Look at each loss in the left column of Table #2 and assign it a value from 1 to 12. A value of 1 would be a loss of highest importance to you; 12 would be a relatively insignificant loss. You and your partner, if you have one, should each do this exercise separately, then compare results.

Your score:_____   Your partner's score:_____

Reading the results:
If you assigned a much higher value to pregnancy, birthing, and genetic connectedness than to parenting, you are probably not ready to make the move. If one partner has placed a far higher value on genetic-connectedness than the other partner, you also need to think long and carefully before choosing adoption or a "semi-adoption" approach such as artificial insemination. If, for example, an infertile man values genetic-connectedness, even where his fertile wife does not place a high value on it, artificial insemination is not going to provide resolution.

After you have weighed your losses, ask yourself whether living infertile and childfree or adopting comes closer to addressing them. Use this exercise as a general guide only. It is important to understand that this decision is likely to be one of the most difficult you ever make in your life. Consult a variety of resources (see the list at the end of the chapter) and consider options such as counseling.

TABLE #2
CONTRAST OF INFERTILITY AND ADOPTION LOSS

Type of loss	Infertility loss?*	Adoption loss?
1. Easy access to parenthood	Yes	Partially — loss lessened or resolved after family is completed by legal adoption
2. Certainty of outcome — parenthood will be a part of one's life	Yes	Partially — loss lessened or resolved after family is completed by legal adoption
3. Entitlement	Yes	Yes
4. Control	Yes	Yes
5. Privacy	Partial	Yes, loss greater in adoption
6. Physical comfort/control	Yes, where fertility treatment is undertaken	No
7. Experience of pregnancy	Yes	Yes
8. Experience of giving birth and nursing	Yes	Yes, but partial if adoptive mother nurses
9. Connectedness— sharing a socially sanctioned rite of passage	Yes, in adoption	Yes, but loss is lessened
10. Genetic connected ness to the child	Yes, even in egg and sperm donation, for infertile parent	Yes, unless relative adoption
11. Jointly conceived child	Yes, even in egg and sperm donation	Yes, but where child is unrelated, loss between adopters is equal for both
12. Opportunity to parent a child	Yes	No, loss fully resolved by adoption

*Infertility losses will also extend to those who choose not to adopt. **Note:** Losses 4, 7, 8, 10, 11, and 12 were identified by Patricia Irwin Johnston and are included here with her permission. For a fuller discussion of these, see Johnston's *Adopting After Infertility*, listed in the Resource Guide.

completed, it can be very difficult to have to explain such choices to a child years later.

c. RESOURCES FOR COPING WITH UNRESOLVED INFERTILITY ISSUES

Analyzing losses, grieving, and simply being sick and tired of the limbo of infertility treatment can all be clues that it is time for you to move on to decision-making. Some find it simple to say "enough is enough." Many of us, however, need outside help in making this momentous decision or in evaluating our readiness to make it. If you are uncertain whether you have resolved your infertility issues sufficiently to proceed to adoption, there are many resources available which offer guidance:

(a) Join RESOLVE or Infertility Awareness Association of Canada (IAAC). These non-profit organizations provide help in obtaining and getting through infertility treatment and all stages of decision-making. Self-help groups, education, newsletters, community and legislative advocacy on infertility issues are offered. See the Resource Guide for further information.

(b) Read about infertility issues. There are excellent books on infertility and making the transition to adoption; some are listed at the end of the chapter.

(c) Talk to people who have moved from infertility to adoption or who have opted to live childfree. Ask them to tell you their stories. RESOLVE, IAAC, and adoptive parent groups are good places to network for peer consultation.

(d) Consult a qualified, independent infertility and adoption counselor. For those stuck on the infertility treatment treadmill, it may help to obtain professional assistance. Just obtaining a sounding-board can help. Most large cities have counselors with experience in this field. To get a referral, consult RESOLVE, IAAC, adoption agencies in your community, or adoptive parent support groups. When you get your referral, find out if the counselor has had experience in infertility issues before committing to counseling. It is important to have a counselor who understands how debilitating the disability of infertility can be. Couples should be counseled together. The counseling process is usually brief, and for those who feel it is time to make a decision, time very well spent.

d. PROVING INFERTILITY FOR ADOPTION PURPOSES

You have decided that you are ready to move on to adoption and have learned that you need to prove that you are infertile to be eligible for certain options. For some, with years of unsuccessful treatment behind them, this is a simple matter of getting a letter from the infertility specialist. But what if the cause of your infertility was never identified or you couldn't afford treatment?

If you are adopting through an agency, ask if they require proof of infertility. Some countries prefer that international adopters be infertile and in that case, proof may be needed. If so, for a couple, the easiest method is to obtain a notarized letter from your primary care physician saying that you are infertile. Because pregnancy rates drop rapidly after 18 months of trying, it is generally agreed that those who do not become pregnant within 18 months can be properly defined as infertile. If you have been trying to conceive for less than at least two years without any infertility evaluation, however, consider investing in a basic infertility workup (a medical assessment of the cause of your infertility). While, contrary to the popular myth, infertile people rarely conceive after adoption, some who have not pursued pregnancy for very long before adopting occasionally do manage to conceive.

If you have received a diagnosis of infertility, providing a notarized letter in writing stating this from your doctor is sufficient. It is *not* necessary to undergo treatment to prove infertility for adoption purposes, although evidence of treatment can, of course, also be used to prove that you are infertile.

Some adopters are actually fertile but, because they carry genes for a serious condition such as Duchenne's muscular dystrophy or because they have a condition which makes pregnancy dangerous such as multiple sclerosis or paraplegia, choose not to attempt biological parenthood. Many agencies and some countries that require proof of infertility will accept instead a letter from your doctor stating why pregnancy for you would be difficult, dangerous, or likely to produce a child with serious health problems. If this is your situation, make sure you ask whether this would be acceptable before deciding you are not eligible for a program which demands proof of infertility.

Single people are generally not expected to demonstrate infertility. If you are permitted to adopt as a single person your fertility should not be an issue. However, any fertile adopters may be asked to refrain from becoming pregnant as a condition of their adoption agreement. Some agencies ask adopters to promise not to seek biological parenthood during the adoption process, even before receiving referral of a child. A private agreement with birth parents in an independent adoption might also provide that the adoptive family be infertile and not seek pregnancy. In such a case, if adopters knowingly sought or achieved pregnancy in contravention of the agreement, it is possible that the agreement could be voided.

e. DEMONSTRATING ADOPTION READINESS TO ADOPTION PROFESSIONALS

Increasingly, adopters are required to undergo a home study before receiving referral and placement of a child. Social workers will want to verify that infertile adopters have sufficiently resolved their infertility prior to adopting. However, not all social workers are trained or experienced in this area of assessment. Some have unrealistic expectations for adoptive parents, expecting that all issues of loss be put wholly behind the family. Since many losses are common both to infertility and adoption, such expectations are unreasonable. You may feel the losses acutely and yet be ready to adopt. If you have gone through a soul searching decision-making process, acknowledging your feelings of anger and pain, and if you have allowed yourself to grieve for the losses you have suffered and still wish to be parents more than you wish to be childless, you are probably ready to adopt.

Some agencies and social workers feel that adopters should have stopped infertility treatment some time before seeking to adopt. This may or may not be a reasonable expectation in today's world of infertility and adoption. If you have selected an agency which tells you there is a six-year waiting period for the kind of placement you are seeking, it would seem unreasonable to expect you to refrain from seeking any treatment during that time. On the other hand, because infertility treatment is so expensive and exhausting, physically and emotionally, it is understandable that adoption professionals consider those undergoing invasive treatments and surgeries may not have the resources to cope with the equally challenging process of adoption.

One area where adopters have difficulty is persuading adoption professionals that they are ready to proceed with adoption very shortly after receiving a diagnosis of infertility, unsuccessful treatment, or losing a pregnancy. Often, infertile people start considering adoption as an alternative very early on. The couple who has been mulling over adoption while undergoing drug therapies and surgeries may well be emotionally ready to choose adoption the very day they learn that a treatment has failed. Of course, they may just as possibly be stunned and devastated and unready to consider any action rationally for months. Equally, the couple who ceased treatment after ten years and turns slowly to adoption may still be obsessed with conception, even though they have lived with a poor prognosis for a long time.

Every family is different and comes to terms with crisis and loss in its own way. Adopters are individuals and should not be subjected to a standardized assessment process, required to meet objective tests of readiness such as living with an infertility diagnosis for a set period of time. Here are some suggestions for demonstrating adoption readiness to professionals:

(a) Discuss your decision-making process. Be frank about how you got from infertility to adoption. If you couldn't afford infertility diagnosis and/or treatment, discuss how you feel about that and why you chose not to pursue it.

(b) List the help you have sought in arriving at your decision, such as books you have read, counseling you have received, membership in a support group. If friends and family have helped you move toward adoption, describe this.

(c) If you are still in infertility treatment, but feel ready to adopt, be prepared to discuss how you can handle both. Even if ceasing treatment is not required in your adoption process, you may be expected to remain committed to adoption, even if you become pregnant. If you are not in treatment, but are having unprotected intercourse, it is wise to say so, when asked. Since many families aim to have more than one child, seeking biological parenthood while trying to adopt may be acceptable. In any event, honesty is always recommended in adoption.

RESOURCE GUIDE

1. Books on infertility

Borg, Susan. *When Pregnancy Fails.* New York: Bantam Books, 1989.

Johnston, Patricia Irwin. *Adopting After Infertility.* Indianapolis, IN: Perspectives Press, 1992.

_____. *Understanding: A Guide to Impaired Fertility for Family and Friends.* Indianapolis, IN: Perspectives Press, 1983.

Mason, Mary Martin. *The Miracle Seekers.* Fort Wayne, IN: Perspectives Press, 1987. (Out of print now, but may be available at your library or from your adoptive parent support group.)

2. Support organizations

- RESOLVE, Inc.
  1310 Broadway
  Sommerville, MA 02144
  (617) 623-0744

- Infertility Awareness Association of Canada
  104 – 1785 Alta Vista Drive
  Ottawa, Ontario
  K1G 3Y6
  1-800-263-2929; (613) 728-8968

TIPS

Deciding to move into adoption requires skills in assessment and decision-making that we may not have when we face the crisis of infertility. There are excellent books about evaluation, decision-making, and transitions that were not written especially for infertile families, but that do offer excellent guidance in coping with life crises. Beyond the boundaries of a topic, resources may exist which can shed new light on the original issue. Here are some resources to get you started:

Bridges, William. *Transitions: Making Sense of Life's Changes.* Reading, MA: Addison-Wesley Publishing Company, 1980.

Carroll, John S. *Decision Research: A Field Guide.* Newbury Park, CA: Sage Publishing, 1990.

Kaufman, Roger. *Identifying and Solving Problems: A Systems Approach.* La Jolla, CA: University Associates, Inc., 1976.

Lippitt, Ronald. *The Dynamics of Planned Change.* New York: Harcourt, Brace and Company, 1958.

5
EXPLORING YOUR OPTIONS

a. IDENTIFYING ISSUES: WHO CAN ADOPT?

Today, most would-be parents who meet their state's definition of who can adopt will be allowed to parent a child. There are, however, a few exceptions. People with criminal records, especially serious ones, may not be permitted to adopt. If you have a minor criminal conviction or have pleaded guilty to a minor offense, you may be able to adopt. A gray area exists where someone is the subject of an accusation that is never substantiated or taken to court, such as a report of child abuse to a child welfare authority. People with serious disabilities or who suffer from life-threatening illnesses may be turned down. On the other hand, wheelchair users and people with multiple sclerosis have successfully adopted.

Where the law is silent, the decision-maker may be the person who does the home study and recommends for or against approval of the adoption in court. Adopters are sometimes turned away by an agency whose criteria they don't meet before a home study is done. Unfortunately, some give up at this stage without exploring other options, such as another agency or independent adoption. The few who receive an unfavorable recommendation in a home study are often unaware that it is possible to appeal. (See chapter 12 for a discussion of how to do this.)

1. Traits that broaden or narrow your options

There is often an unspoken hierarchy in the minds of adoption professionals about who constitutes the "best" adoptive families. Different agencies and individuals have different hierarchies, however. An agency closely affiliated to a church may place membership in that church high on its list of desirable traits. An agency that places mostly non-white children from developing countries may value multi-cultural experience and maturity most highly. For some services, adopters' ability to pay may figure highly in their desirability.

You should be aware of your "strengths" and "weaknesses" regarding different adoption choices. Table #3 sets out traits that will affect your adoption choices. No single trait will make you acceptable or unacceptable as an adoptive parent for every kind of child. For example, a "typical" affluent adoptive married couple might be rejected and a single older woman chosen as a parent for a young girl with a history of sexual abuse.

Some adoption realities should be acknowledged. An affluent, childless, church-going, single wage earner couple, between the ages of 25 and 35, married once for five years or more, has the most choices. Those of us who don't fit the traditional societal norm of a "good parent," people I refer to as "non-traditional adopters," face more barriers. The lower your income the more likely you are to be precluded from a choice because it is too costly. Still, most people have several options to consider. Identifying what those are is the task.

2. Turning "weaknesses" into strengths

For some of us, such as the couple described above, it is hard to make an adoption choice because there are so many possibilities. But for an older couple with prior marriages and children, or for homosexuals and lesbians, the choices will be harder because they will be limited. In each case, however, adoption is possible. As lawyers and advertisers know, every issue has an "up" as well as a "down" side. So-called "weaknesses" can prove to be strengths.

In most non-relative adoptions, as part of the home study process you will be asked to write your "autobiography" or

TABLE #3
TRAITS THAT AFFECT ADOPTION CHOICES

Each of these traits will affect your choices and how adoption professionals see you. In some cases, whether these traits widen or narrow your options depends on the kind of adoption you seek. For each, the task is to demonstrate that the trait enhances or at least doesn't interfere with your ability to parent a child.

Marital status
Married couple
Up to one prior divorce for each
Two or more prior divorces
Length of marriage
Single
Unmarried couple

Sexual orientation
Heterosexual
Gay or lesbian
Bisexual
Age
Under 25
Between 25 - 30
Between 30 - 35
Between 35 - 40
Between 40 - 45
Over 45
More than 10 years age difference between members of couple

Health
Good health
Mild chronic illness/condition
Moderate chronic illness/condition
Severe chronic illness/condition

Disability
Mild disability
Moderate disability
Severe disability

Racial descent/culture
European
Asian
East Indian
European
Latino
Interracial couple
Jewish
Multiracial (one or more adopters is of multiracial descent)
Native American
Other (i.e., Polynesian, Middle Eastern)
U.S.-born citizen
Naturalized citizen

Religion
Roman Catholic
Protestant
Jewish
Islamic
Hindu
Buddhist
Minority faith (i.e., Bahai, Sufi, Scientology)

TABLE #3 — Continued

Employment

Professional/managerial

Relevant to adoption (i.e. social work, mental/physical health, work with children)

Non-decision–making

Long hours

Part time/Flexibility of hours

Ability of one member of couple to stay home with child

Income

Level of income

Dependent on one or two earners

Certainty (tenure, permanency etc.)

Family makeup

Biological children

Other adopted children

Live with other extended family members

Support system

Extended family

Network of friends

Child care options in community

Living situation

Own a home

Own a townhouse/condo

Rent a home

Rent a townhouse/apartment

Number of bedrooms

Community

Cultural/racial diversity

Urban

Rural

Suburban

Financial health

Assets and debts

Life Insurance

Health insurance for child

Coverage from time of custody

Coverage from finalization of adoption

Criminal record

Convicted/pleaded guilty to felony (especially drug, child abuse, sexual assault charge)

Convicted/pleaded guilty to minor charge

Charged with offense or reported to child welfare agency, but never prosecuted tell about yourselves. This information is incorporated into the final home study, and paraphrased or quoted by the person preparing the study. Additionally, in an independent adoption, adopters are usually chosen by birth parents initially on the basis of a personal statement — a few paragraphs describing the adoptive family, why they seek to adopt, and what they offer a child. What is it they and other adoption decision-makers are seeking?

Adoption decision-makers, from agency professionals to birth parent, look for certain characteristics in any adoptive family they select:

(a) Stability (financial, social, emotional)

(b) Permanence (adopters will continue to be there
      for the child)

(c) Love (adopters can and will love the child)

(d) Community (adopters have a caring support system
      that will embrace the child)

(e) Competence (adopters are competent to raise a child)

(f) Moral/ethical character (adopters are good
      human beings)

What each decision-maker accepts as evidence of good adopter material may vary. As your own advocate, you need to be prepared to show how you can provide these to your child. What traits and experience do you have which demonstrate your fitness to parent the kind of child you are looking for? A trait that may appear to be a drawback at first, such as age, may be an advantage if your life experience has given you a good income, patience, and wisdom. What is there in your background that might limit your parenting ability? Address the issue directly. A wheelchair user, far from being handicapped as a parent, may bring added resourcefulness as a result of having to function in a world designed for the able-bodied. Exercise #2 at the end of this chapter is designed to help you evaluate and present yourself to decision-makers as a prospective parent.

b. WHAT KIND OF CHILD IS AVAILABLE TO ME?

Throughout this section it is important to remember that you do have choices. The most effective approach is to match your own current interests and experience with your adoption choice. In general, adopters who choose the kind of child and adoption experience that conforms with their own experience, beliefs, and interests make the happiest and most successful parents.

1. Boy or girl?

Most American and Canadian parents say they would prefer a boy as their first born, but adopters, as a rule, choose girls more often than boys. With the exception of a few countries such as China and India, it is more difficult to adopt a girl than a boy. One reason is that more boys are available; as well, those girls that are free to be adopted are more sought after.

Some agencies and countries do not allow adopters to specify gender, especially if they are childless. In independent adoption, a plan is usually made prior to birth and the adoptive family accepts the child — boy or girl. In independent international adoption, it is often possible to specify gender; however, that often means a longer wait for the child sought.

As you weigh your options, examine your views on gender carefully. Are you making unsupported assumptions about which kind of child is "better" or easier to raise? If you can bring yourself to accept either sex, you are likely to become a parent sooner.

2. Healthy infants

Newborn babies of European descent are in the greatest demand and shortest supply of all adoptable children in the United States. Often, the goal of the adopters is simply to parent the healthiest, youngest infant available. Understandably, they wish their child to be as close a replacement as possible for a desired biological child. There is nothing wrong with this desire. But if unexamined, it can lead to problems later on.

Most newborn adoptees are placed in adoptive homes when only a few days old, on the assumption that they are healthy infants. However, good health and freedom from medical problems can never be guaranteed. Some adopters wish to parent only babies in good health and make that part of their adoption agreement. Where high fees are charged, it may seem fair to expect a healthy baby in return. But some health problems cannot be diagnosed at birth. Fetal alcohol effects, autism, hyperactivity, developmental problems, deafness, and other conditions may surface years later.

Before you pay a huge premium for a "healthy newborn," you need to understand that a minority of these children, like any others, will eventually be diagnosed with those or other conditions. There is absolutely no way, through agency or independent adoption, even where you work closely with the birth mother and she receives good prenatal care and testing, that you can guarantee a perfectly healthy child. Competent and ethical agencies working closely with birth parents with known medical histories still make no such guarantees. Realizing this truth before you adopt can help you to consider more options than just the "healthy newborn" option.

Adoptable newborns may be of minority race. Some adopters mistakenly believe that there are many such babies available, but healthy newborns of any race are in the smallest category of adoptable children. In non-white communities, birth mothers who place a child for adoption often turn first to their extended families. Some babies, especially biracial children, are placed for formal adoption, however. Who is chosen to parent them is controversial.

Some agencies will place minority newborns with any acceptable adopters, whatever their race. Others place these children only with same-race parents. In some cases, newborns are put into foster care until a permanent same race family can be found. In independent adoptions, minority birth mothers have chosen both same-race and transracial adopters to parent their children.

If you are a minority single person or couple, you can almost certainly find a newborn minority baby to adopt. While stories persist of agencies who turn away eligible minority adopters because they don't have professional jobs or appear to be a "good" adoptive family to the white agency worker who does the home study, excellent resources for minority adopters do exist. Many agencies specialize in minority placement. For Native or part-Native American families, there are also many resources. Asian American families will find few same-race children placed for adoption domestically, but are likely to receive preference in adopting children from Asian countries. Where in-race placement is a high value for an agency, efforts are more likely to be made to make adoption affordable to qualified minority adopters. Agencies based in the southern U.S. often place more minority infants than do agencies elsewhere. See the Resource Guide for suggestions.

If you are of European descent and seek a minority baby, it is important to examine your motivations. If you don't do this now, you can be sure you'll be asked to later. In our highly race-conscious society, it is never believable to say "race makes no difference to me." Ask yourself the following questions:

(a) How do you feel about adults of other races?

(b) Do you live in a multi-cultural neighborhood?

(c) Are you prepared to move to such a neighborhood?

(d) Do you have friends of different races?

(e) Are you considering transracial adoption only because you feel that you are more likely to succeed in adopting if you seek a minority child than if you seek a white one?

(f) Are you prepared to be a non-white family and graft a minority onto your family tree?

(g) Are you interested in a minority culture?

(h) Have you acted on this interest before now?

(i) Are you prepared to accept the high visibility your family will have?

(j) Are you prepared to make a considerable effort to preserve your child's heritage and to participate in the community and culture of origin?

You should be able to answer yes to most of these except (e) if you are adopting transracially and be prepared to answer these questions for adoption professionals, birth parents, and judges. Think about what steps you can take to integrate two or more cultures in your family. This is a choice you should make only if you are prepared to defend it publicly.

3. Older infants, toddlers, and preschoolers

A few years ago, any healthy child over one or two years old was defined as "hard to place." Today, most states don't consider a healthy child under five or six hard to place. Many adopters, faced with a long wait for a newborn, decide to seek an older child. If the child is healthy, without siblings needing same-family placement, legally free, and not a known victim of serious abuse, finding parents is not a difficult task. The same goes for small children with minor or correctable handicaps. Still, the wait for these children is likely to be much shorter than for a newborn.

An advantage of adopting such a child is that the issue of birth parent rights may be resolved already and the risk of birth parents changing their minds low to nonexistent. To find such a child it is almost always necessary to go through an adoption agency, public or private. Because many public agencies have so many older special needs children in their care, they often refer younger children to private agencies for placement. Again, race is a factor just as it is for newborns.

Even babies only a few months old have important separation issues to deal with. The older a child is, the longer his or her past. They have lost important attachments. A child may have been abused or suffer from a condition not apparent at the time of referral. These children are usually eligible for adoption subsidies. If so, it is important to obtain the subsidy before you finalize the adoption, since it may be impossible to get one later. These adoptions are generally less expensive than newborn adoptions even without a subsidy.

4. Special needs children

"Special needs" is a state-defined category which means a child who is hard to place in that state. Most often, these are older children, sibling groups, and children with severe physical or emotional disabilities. A few may be infants. Some children have special needs simply by virtue of spending years in inadequate or temporary care. Not every child with a disability is hard to place. Some states have waiting lists of adopters hoping to parent an infant with Down's syndrome.

Many parents have adopted a special needs child and found the experience so positive they have gone on to adopt more. Often these parents already have biological or other adopted children. Overall, however, special needs adoptions are more likely to fail. About 10% of these children will eventually be returned to foster care.

Interestingly, the most successful adoptions involve working class adopters, often younger and less educated. Successful adopters tend to be people who can love and accept a child who will never be a high achiever. Special needs adoptions are also more likely to succeed where foster parents are the adopters. If you are interested in exploring adoption of a special needs child, the best avenue open to you may be to become a licensed foster parent. See also the foster/adopt section later in this chapter.

5. Children available internationally

Newborn babies are seldom available through international adoption, but it is often possible to adopt infants under six months old. If you are prepared to adopt a child under one year, there are many options available.

Race is an important issue to consider before adopting internationally. Few countries bar transracial placement. Some adopters have little or no idea of the racial backgrounds of available children and are surprised to find that they have adopted transracially, after the fact. If race is important to you and you seek a Caucasian baby, you should adopt domestically. Even a European country may be placing primarily non-European babies for adoption. Because race is an issue worldwide, some countries place only children of mixed or different race from that of the majority culture. Many Romanian adoptees were of Gypsy heritage, for example, and Bulgarian babies adopted internationally are usually of part-African descent. Adopters may be uncomfortable about their racial feelings. But you owe it to yourself and your child to be honest about these feelings before you take any irrevocable steps.

Latin America is a good case in point. Many Latin American adoptees are of mixed race. Racial blends of Native (Indian), Southern European (Spanish or Portuguese), and African are common. The skin color of multiracial children often changes as they grow up, sometimes growing darker. A newborn might appear white in a photo, but that child at two years may be of obviously non-white descent.

I would like to be able to say that most adopters can rise above the issue of skin color once they have that child in their arms. Unfortunately, I cannot. The fact is that some adopters are incapable of loving a child of another race and have abandoned partly completed adoptions because of this. Understandably, countries where this has happened may come to view North American adopters negatively. Some adopters feel that because international adoption facilitators charge high fees, they should guarantee the child's race. But even if that were desirable, facilitators rarely know the child's racial background. A high fee is no guarantee of racial composition. In countries such as Colombia or Brazil where most people are of mixed race, a guarantee of whiteness may signal an illegal adoption.

A high proportion of internationally adopted children prove to have special needs. They may suffer from one or several problems such as failure to thrive, developmental delays, spina bifida, hepatitis B, and other chronic poverty-related diseases. Some children are free for adoption only because they have serious health problems which their biological parents had no resources to address. Many American and Canadian families have adopted these children and some have done remarkably well once they have had enough to eat and adequate health care. But many problems are lifelong. While the child may do far better in an adoptive home than if left in the country of origin, success may mean high school graduation, not Yale Law School.

One factor parents need to consider when adopting older children from other countries is the issue of language. Learning a new language, while easier for children than for adults, is difficult. These children, in addition to having special needs, must become accustomed to a new family and culture all at once. Families who have had this experience can offer useful advice if your child is school-aged. They can help you learn what resources your community offers, such as English as a second language instruction, to help integrate your child into your community, advice on how to help your child retain the first language, and how to locate community resources. Before choosing to adopt an older, non-English speaking child, talk to parents who have done so and envision how you will overcome the obstacles to communication.

A significant factor to consider in choosing to adopt one of these children is your financial resources. Children who have never been in the care of a U.S. state agency are unlikely to meet a state's definition of "special needs," and will not be eligible for an adoption subsidy. Since many of these children require extensive medical and therapeutic intervention, you need to plan for how you will pay for it. Some family health care policies provide adequate coverage. Others, especially those which rule out coverage for "pre-existing conditions," will not. Most U.S. states do not require health insurers to provide equal coverage for adopted and biological children. Because health care policy is changing rapidly in the U.S., stay up to date on the issue and know how you will pay for related items such as extensive counseling or physical therapy.

In deciding for or against international adoption, ask yourself the same questions listed under minority adoption. And to those questions add some questions about culture:

(a) Are you interested in the culture of the country you are considering adopting from?

(b) Have you acted on such an interest before?

(c) Do you know people from the culture?

(d) Is this culture represented in your community?

(e) Do you speak the language of this culture?

(f) Have you ever studied a foreign language?

(g) Do you have friends from other countries and cultures?

(h) Do you enjoy vacationing in other countries and if so, do you explore the culture or do you prefer to stick to tourist areas?

(i) Have you ever wanted to explore any of these possibilities before?

If you answer no to more than a few of these questions, you should reconsider your plans. International adoption works best for adopters who are genuinely interested in the culture of their child. Sometimes adopters have little background in other cultures but are thrilled to have an opportunity to get to know one first hand. For them, international adoption satisfies several dreams at once — it provides the opportunity to parent as well as to travel and reach out to a new country and new cultural experiences. There are those, however, who feel uncomfortable outside their own country and have little interest in other cultures and these may not make the best parents of internationally adopted children.

c. WHAT KINDS OF ADOPTION ARE AVAILABLE TO ME?

1. Agency adoption

(a) Public agencies

A public agency is almost always the least expensive route to adoption. Fees are minimal to non-existent and subsidies are often available for adoption expenses, health care, and other services. Today's public agencies place children in virtually every kind of family, so for non-traditional adopters, a public agency may be especially appealing. Minority race and culture are advantages. However, some public agencies are mandated by state law or by their internal policies not to place transracially. If you are a non-traditional adopter and/or of limited means, and willing to accept the challenge of parenting an older child or sibling group, this is a strong option.

If you are considering special needs adoption, your first step should be to contact a public agency. Although private agencies may lower fees and waive eligibility criteria for special needs children, public agencies will usually be even less expensive and more likely to offer knowledgeable post-placement support and services, as well as assistance in obtaining adoption subsidies and other financial aid. However, because of the increase of children coming into public care, many public agencies are greatly over-extended and have contracted out most of their adoption functions to private agencies. If so, your public agency can direct you to the private agencies they work with.

(b) Private agencies

Private agency adoption offers many advantages. The agency takes responsibility for the adoption process, and the number of people and institutions you must deal with is minimized. Some fees may be refundable or payable only on successful completion of the adoption. Agencies are government-regulated. Some countries only permit international adoption of their children when carried out by a licensed agency.

If your objective is to adopt a newborn Caucasian infant, traditional agency adoption may not meet your needs. Criteria are likely to be restrictive, waiting lists long, and fees high. If you are willing to take some of the risks of independent adoption described in the next section, however, there are agencies which can help you through "designated adoption" programs. These combine the freedom of independent adoption with supports available through agency adoption.

As domestic infant agency adoption has slowed, more U.S. agencies direct their efforts at helping families adopt healthy and special needs infants from other countries. The agency rarely acquires custody of the child. Agencies with large programs overseas are able to provide many services to adopters that are not available through non-agency facilitated international adoption. Because international adoption is complicated, frustrating, and subject to problems at the best of times, agency facilitation may be a better option than the independent route for most adopters. Unfortunately, restrictive agency eligibility criteria may close this option to non-traditional adopters, especially when added to eligibility restrictions imposed by the countries on adopter age, fertility, and marital status.

Agencies screen adopter applicants to ensure they meet eligibility criteria set by the agency. Different programs may have different criteria. A program placing Caucasian newborns, for example, could be restricted to childless married couples, between 25 and 35, with no prior divorces. Yet the same agency may place waiting children with any adopter, single or married, who meets the state's definition of "who may adopt" and receives a favorable home study recommendation.

Private agencies often have small staffs and make relatively few placements each year. They discourage long waiting lists by being selective about who they accept as prospective parents. Some agencies make fewer than 10 placements per year, while others make hundreds.

Programs placing toddlers and preschoolers through an agreement with a public agency may be offered. Some private agencies license and place children in foster homes and supervise placements through an agreement with a public agency, as well as place special needs children in adoptive families.

2. Independent adoption

Any adoption conducted without an agency is an independent (also known as private) adoption. Two-thirds of newborn adoptions in the United States are independent as birth mothers choose to place an infant independently more often than through an agency. Except for the few states that ban private placement, the option is widely available.

On their own or with a facilitator's help, adopters locate the birth parents, usually before the birth of the child, make an adoption plan with them directly or through an intermediary, and carry out the adoption shortly after the child's birth. A home study is obtained from a legally valid source in the state. Public and private agencies may do home studies for independent adopters. Today many services are offered to help independent adopters become parents. Unless the service is a licensed child-placing agency, however, it may not be subject to government scrutiny.

Adopters must decide on the degree of contact they wish to have with the birth parents. Most employ an attorney or facilitation service to screen birth parents and mediate prospective contact and issues, such as medical or other fees to be paid on behalf of the birth mother.

The common approach to finding birth parents is to place advertisements asking pregnant women to place their unborn child in a certain family. Not everyone is comfortable with this approach to adoption and many states have banned or restricted adoption advertising. While the issue is controversial, many birth parents and adopters feel firmly that this was a good choice for them and that banning independent adoption, as some adoption professionals wish to do, would eliminate the choice most responsible for widening birth parent options in adoption.

Other birth parents have become disillusioned with independent placements and have joined together to seek a ban on them. Some birth mothers now feel they were pressured into making unwise adoption plans at a time in their lives when they were vulnerable to such pressure. Whichever view is held, most agree that there is more opportunity for abuses and unhappy endings with independent than with agency adoptions, so extra care is needed going about it. Before choosing this option, expose yourself to the views of those who oppose it. Whether you agree with them or not, they will introduce you to important issues you might not otherwise encounter that can help you make the best choice for your family.

Some adopters have very positive experiences with independent adoption. Others have found it much more problematic. Birth mothers more often choose healthy, childless married adopters. Non-traditional adopters such as lesbian couples, singles, or people with disabilities have also been selected, but they are likely to wait longer for a placement.

Costs of independent adoption are beyond prediction and control of adopters, since they generally depend on whether the birth mother has health insurance, whether the pregnancy and delivery are difficult or easy, and if the birth mother has other legitimate expenses adopters need to pay. As more families have chosen independent adoption, adopters and facilitators have increasingly looked outside their own state for birth parents. This usually invokes the Interstate Compact, discussed in chapter 2, and can add time and expense to the process.

Independent international adoption is often the only way some families can adopt healthy infants under one or two years of age. Single parents and those who don't follow a mainstream religion may have a difficult time finding an international agency program that accepts them, although some will. Agencies often prohibit adoption of children more than 40 years younger than the oldest adoptive parent. For families who already have children, biological or adopted, these agency age restrictions may mean a child they are allowed to adopt will be older than children already in the adopters' family.

3. Domestic versus international adoption

Domestic adoption may or may not be a faster route to parenthood than international adoption, but it is almost always easier. You will have far fewer documents to collect and fewer bureaucratic hoops to jump through. The people you deal with will speak English. Even if travel is required, it will not require a passport, visa, great expense, or extensive preparation. If you adopt out of state, caring for your child temporarily in a Holiday Inn will be much easier than in a Bolivian hotel room. Your child will almost certainly be reasonably healthy, and if old enough to speak, will speak English. Time away from work needed to process the adoption will be short. If you run into difficulties, resources to help you cope are available. You can contact your agency, an attorney, and a doctor easily. You will be able to use your leave from work to bond with your child in your home. If you are adopting an older special needs child, you may be eligible for financial assistance.

Contrast this picture with international adoption, where you will need to collect many documents, have them notarized, verified by a local and/or state authority, translated and then authenticated by the country's embassy or consulate. Then you or your agency will have to get the documents to the attorney or intermediary in your child's country or hand carry them when you travel.

You will have little or no control over timing. Identifying a child may take months or even years. If you are lucky you will be given a photo and some information on which to base a decision to accept or reject a referral. But you may not have that opportunity. Once a child is identified, you could still wait months or years until you travel. Some adopters, in Peru or Romania for example, have traveled without having a child identified for them, hoping to find one once they were in the country. For many of these people, adoptions take months to accomplish and some have returned home without a child. Even a well-planned international adoption can require a stay of several months in a foreign country. Although the new Family Leave Act allows some adopters up to 12 weeks of unpaid leave, many cannot afford a 12-week break from their paychecks. And some international adoptions take even longer.

On the plus side, international adoption can be exciting, enriching, and fascinating far beyond the experience of domestic adoption. You may have the chance to travel to exotic places, make new friends, explore a new culture, and form bonds that will last a lifetime. For many of us, these advantages more than offset the drawbacks to international adoption. In one act we have transformed our little nuclear families into international ones.

4. Foster adopt programs

Some agencies have developed programs that attempt to combine foster care and adoption with a view to shortening the time children spend in temporary care. These are known as foster adopt or permanency planning programs. Licensed foster parents and agency clients willing to be licensed are eligible. Following licensing and foster parent training, they are referred a child who has come into foster care. If they accept the referral, the foster parents then work with agency staff and biological families to develop a parenting plan for this child. The goal is to have a permanent plan in place within a short time, usually less than 18 months. During that time efforts are made to assist the biological family to parent the child, if possible. Occasionally such efforts are successful and the child returns to them. If so, the foster parents will be referred another child. If the biological parents are unable to parent, they may be encouraged to work with the foster family to plan for the child's future. An open adoption might result especially if the child is older and the foster and biological families work out a plan for visitation and contact.

These programs differ from ordinary foster care in several ways. First, the foster family has a clear goal of adopting this child, so the placement will reflect the kind of child the adopters are seeking. Another difference is that this process can be less adversarial. By including the biological family in planning for a degree of openness, they may feel comfortable enough with the placement to accept termination of their parental rights instead of opposing it through a long court action. If the placement doesn't work out for the adopters, the fact that it is a foster placement can allow the parties to end the relationship without the sense of failure that a disrupted adoption brings.

d. CHOOSING THE OPTION THAT'S RIGHT FOR YOU

If you are still not certain about which option to choose, you can do some more research. Call the AFA HELP line and talk with a volunteer. Talk to parents who have chosen any of the options you are considering. Make a list of questions to ask them. An adoptive parent group can make such referrals. Take an extension class at a university or college in child development and other parenting issues. Attend an adoption fair. (If your community sponsors these, they are likely to be held in November, which is national adoption month in the United States and Canada.)

You might interview one or two agencies briefly by telephone, explain that you are considering agency adoption, and ask them to give you ten minutes of their time to discuss the pros and cons. You could become a licensed foster parent, or you could volunteer in a program that involves contact with special needs children.

Putting the advantages and disadvantages of each choice in writing can help you make a decision you can live with. Interesting studies have been done on people who make a balance sheet of pros and cons before coming to a life decision. These list-makers end up happier with their decisions and more likely to stick with them. Formally reviewing and evaluating your options can show you gaps in your knowledge of the issues. You can do some early contingency planning. If you have weighted your options, you'll have a second and a third choice at hand if your first doesn't work out. Another benefit of putting choices in writing is that sometimes, even when an option has everything going for it on paper, it doesn't "feel" right. That can be a sign that factors exist that you aren't consciously taking into account but that are important to you.

If the choice doesn't work out, what will you do? Try making a risk assessment of each option. Imagine a "worst case scenario" for any choice and plan a way out for yourself in advance if the scenario occurs. You may never have to use it, but if you do — it's there. Exercise #2 will help you in this decision-making process.

EXERCISE #2
SELF-EVALUATION

Make a chart setting out your strengths and weaknesses as prospective parents with respect to the six parenting fundamentals. Refer to Table #3 for traits that affect adoption. Then write a personal statement, no more than one page long, demonstrating what you, through your personal traits and the life experience you have accumulated, can bring to the task of parenting a child. Think about the kind of child you wish to parent. How does your background make you a good choice to parent such a child?

RESOURCE GUIDE

1. Single adopters

- Committee for Single Adoptive Parents
  Box 15084
  Chevy Chase, MD 20815

- Singles With Adopted Kids (SWAK)
  4116 Washington Road, #202
  Kenosha, WI 53144

- Single Mothers by Choice
  P.O. Box 1642
  Gracie Square Station
  New York, NY 10028
  (212) 988-0993

2. Gay and lesbian adopters

- Chain of Life
  P.O. Box 8081
  Berkeley, CA 94707

Dahl, Judy. *River of Promise: Two Women's Story of Love and Adoption.* San Diego, CA: Luramedia, 1989.

Martin, April. *The Lesbian and Gay Parenting Handbook: Creating and Raising our Families.* New York: HarperCollins, 1993.

3. Jewish adopters

- Stars of David
  #2 Wenonah Avenue
  Rockaway, NJ 07866
  (201) 627-7752

4. Native American adopters

- National American Indian Adoption Service
  Three Feathers Associates
  P.O. Box 5508
  Norman, OK 73070
  (405) 360-2919

- Native American Adoption Resource Exchange
  Council of Three Rivers
  American Indian Center
  200 Charles Street
  Pittsburgh, PA 15238
  (412) 782-4457

5. African American adopters

- One Church, One Child
  1317 Winewood Boulevard
  Building 8, Room 312
  Tallahassee, FL 32399-0700

This organization helps African American families adopt African American children acrosss the United States. Check your community for a local chapter.

6. Adopters with disabilities

At present there is no national organization representing adopters with disabilities. Sydney Jacobs, a wheelchair user and adoptive mother, is willing to act as a resource for disabled adopters and would-be adopters interested in forming a network. She can be reached at 2302 Lackawanna Street, Adelphi, MD 20783.

7. Additional adoption resources

- AASK America Adoption Exchange
  657 Mission Street, Suite 601
  San Francisco, CA 94105
  1-800-23-AASK
  (415) 543-2275

- Down's Syndrome Adoption Exchange
  5600 Midchester Avenue
  White Plains, NY 10606
  (914) 428-1236

- Jewish Children's Adoption Network
  P.O. Box 16544
  Denver, CO 80216
  (303) 573-8113

- National Resource Center for Special Needs Adoption
  Spaulding for Children
  16250 Northland Drive, Suite 120
  Southville, MI 48075
  (313) 443-7080

- National Foster Parents Association
  Information and Services Office
  226 Kilts Drive
  Houston, TX 77024-6214
  (713) 467-1850

This group represents 100,000 foster families in the U.S. It offers families information, support, and services, and advocates on their behalf with local, state, and national governments.

- Pact — An Adoption Alliance (for transracial adoption)
  3315 Sacramento Street, Suite 239
  San Francisco, CA 94118
  (415) 221-8765

Pact is a service helping the adoption triad deal with racial issues. They support and facilitate appropriate independent transracial placements, educate families on racism and how to overcome it, and publish a newsletter. They support the right of birthparents to choose independent transracial adoption.

- Association of Multiethnic Americans (AMEA)
  P.O. Box 191726
  San Francisco, CA 94119-1726
  (510) 523-AMEA

AMEA is a national organization representing individuals of multiethnic/multiracial descent as well as interracial families. It has ties to similar groups in the United States and Canada. AMEA includes adoptive as well as biological interracial families and couples. They support efforts and activities which recognize and affirm the full multiracial identities of individuals and families.

8. Adoptive parent groups

- Latin American Adoptive Families (LAAF)
  40 Upland Road
  Duxbury, MA 02332
  (617) 934-6756

- LAAF in Canada
  2250 Heidi Avenue
  Burlington, Ontario
  L7M 3W4

- Latin American Parents Association
  P.O. Box 4403
  Silver Spring, MD 20904
  (301) 431-3407

These organizations represent families who have adopted or hope to adopt from Central and South America. Newsletters and, in some areas, networking and support groups are available. Fact sheets about adoption for particular countries are available from LAAF.

9. Books and publications

Bartholet, Elizabeth. *Family Bonds: Adoption and the Politics of Parenting.* New York: Houghton Mifflin, 1993.

Bates, J. Douglas. *Gift Children: A Story of Race, Family, and Adoption in a Divided America.* New York: Ticknor & Fields, 1993

Caplan, Lincoln. *An Open Adoption*. New York: Houghton Mifflin, 1990.

Dorris, Michael. *The Broken Cord*. New York: Harper & Row, 1989.

Goldstein, Joseph et al. *Beyond the Best Interests of the Child* (1973) and *In the Best Interests of the Child*. New York: Free Press. 1986

Jewett, Claudia. *Adopting the Older Child*. Boston, MA: Harvard Common Press, 1974.

Krementz, Jill. *How it Feels to be Adopted*. New York: Alfred A. Knopf, 1982.

Register, Cheri. *Are Those Kids Yours?* New York: Free Press, 1990.

Simon, R.J. and H. Altstein. *Transracial Adoptees and Their Families: A Study of Identity and Commitment*. New York: Praeger, 1987.

TIPS

For members of non-traditional faiths, explore whether your church has family support groups or organizations which include adoptive parents. If you are in a small community, contact a branch of your church in a larger one. Church newsletters and magazines may advertise such groups.

6
SETTING YOUR GOALS

a. USING GOAL SETTING IN YOUR ADOPTION PLAN

Most adoptions take over a year to accomplish; many will take two or three and some may take as long as five or ten years. Each, however long or short, can be divided into stages. Every time you reach the end of a stage and move onto the next, you have accomplished a goal. Because of the frustrations and uncertainties inherent in adoption, by dividing your adoption into stages, each with its clearly defined goal, you can bring structure and coherence to the process.

Setting short-term, interim, and long-term goals can help you establish and maintain an adoption plan through a long and often difficult process. These could include plans to —

(a) Survey your options

(b) Interview adoption professionals such as agencies and facilitators

(c) Join an adoptive parent group

(d) Make a plan for financing the adoption

(e) Read books and articles on adoption

(f) Research the country where you plan to adopt from

(g) Become licensed as a foster parent

(h) Volunteer to work with children with special needs

All these are goals within your power to accomplish before you get the referral of your child.

Frame your goals in a way which puts the power in your hands. A poor example of a goal would be: being accepted as a client by an agency. A good example would be: analyzing my options and presenting my strengths as an adopter to an agency. Adopting a baby within a year is a bad choice. Setting aside a specific period of time each week to work on your adoption, identifying tasks that need to be accomplished, and reviewing what has been done is a better choice. Your goals should always be within your grasp, and their success or failure is up to you.

b. A REALITY CHECK: A LOOK AT OPEN ADOPTION

Before you start setting specific goals, take a look at the issue of open adoption. Even as adoption grows more open, there is no general agreement on what is meant by the term "open adoption." What one person sees as open adoption may look like old-fashioned closed adoption to another. Whatever the precise definition, the term signals a scenario in which adoptive parents acknowledge and include their child's birth parents, before and after the adoption, in their planning and to some extent in their family life, whether through indirect mediated contact, correspondence, or actually meeting face to face. But for many prospective adopters, open adoption has a negative, even frightening, connotation. The idea that before you have even become parents, you must consider how to "share" your child with the biological parents is understandably unappealing. However, few open adoptions involve extended, continuous contact between adoptive and birth families. Where families do maintain such contact, it is their free choice. Hard as it may be to believe now, many adopters, and you could be among them, move from fear of even the slightest degree of openness to actively seeking contact with their child's birth parents over the course of adopting their child.

Because of the social stigma, it used to be assumed that birth parents would happily forget about the child they placed for adoption and get on with lives that might be destroyed if it was learned that they had borne an illegitimate child. But it is now widely understood that placing a child for adoption is not a decision that birth parents simply forget about; it is a major event that affects people throughout their lives. The growing popularity of open adoption lends support to the view that many birth parents want some form of contact with, or at least periodic information about, the child they let go.

The old-fashioned closed adoption is dying out in domestic placement. Today, parents adopting a newborn baby in the United States are likely to have been chosen through the exchange of non-identifying information by a birth mother on the basis of photographs of the adoptive family and a personal statement about themselves. There may also be a meeting at which non-identifying information is exchanged, including first names. Throughout the pregnancy, an intermediary maintains contact with both parties and ensures that concerns and information are shared. If all goes well, after the adoption the adoptive family sends photos and information about the child at intervals to birth parents through the intermediary. This process is coming to be known as "semi-open adoption" to distinguish it from adoptions in which birth and adoptive families control and maintain contact without the help of a third party.

Some birth and adoptive parents execute written agreements before the adoption providing for contact. One state makes such agreements enforceable and several others are considering similar laws. Some families prefer to keep visitation arrangements informal.

Even in the most open arrangement, once you have finalized an adoption, you are the only legal parents of your child. You bear the same responsibility for your child's upbringing that any biological parents would have. The biological family, whatever the arrangements for contact, are no longer in any way responsible for raising the child.

Some adopters are so disturbed by the prospect of open adoption that they make an adoption choice exclusively on the basis of how they feel they can best avoid it. Unfortunately, that has led adopters into illegal or fraudulent adoptions or to adopt internationally when they otherwise have no interest in parenting a child of another culture.

Letting go of the safety in the idea of a closed adoption can be difficult. Proponents of wholly closed adoptions still exist and occasionally very open adoptions have led to problems. But the reality is that a majority of infant adoptions in the U.S. are at least partly open today, along with increasing numbers of older child adoptions. You will vastly broaden your choices if you can accept a degree of openness in yours. There are no long-term studies on the effect of open adoption on families, since it is a recent phenomenon. In many cases, just as with families divided by separation and divorce, birth families drift away from the adopted child and contact diminishes or ceases altogether. In other cases contact may be intermittent. Remember, too, that with divorce and remarriage, an ever higher percentage of biological families are dealing with the same issue even more intensely as they negotiate visitation for non-custodial parents and as stepparents feel their way to a relationship with their stepchildren. Complicated families are becoming the rule, not the exception.

Before you make a choice about openness, talk to other adoptive families, especially those who have lived with their arrangement for at least five years. Are they happy with their choice? What are the pros and cons? How has it affected the child? If they could do something different, what would it be? You may be surprised to find that many parents regret not pursuing a more open adoption than they did.

So while you set your goals, consider the degree of openness you are comfortable with. If you settle on a process toward the closed end of the spectrum, consider how you can obtain information about the birth family if it is needed eventually.

c. RECOGNIZING THAT GOALS MAY CHANGE

Keep your goals flexible. If your heart is set on adopting a baby from China and China suddenly closes its borders to adoption, you will have to switch gears if you want to adopt. Your goals will need to change to some degree. You may find that an option that wasn't appealing to you when you started later becomes more attractive.

Maybe you ruled out international adoption because you wanted to adopt only a healthy newborn in the United States. As you learn about this option you find that it has drawbacks you hadn't considered, so you decide to broaden your search. You may have begun to work with an agency that you realize is a poor match for you. At any point along your adoption journey you may need to make changes to your adoption plan. In our case, we worked with three adoption agencies and considered two different countries before settling on an independent adoption in Brazil. Some changes were beyond our control. Others were decisions we made as we became more familiar with adoption issues.

If you plan your process well and do your homework, you can avoid many unnecessary detours and dead ends. However, the volatile nature of today's adoption world virtually guarantees that you will have to redirect your adoption at least once. When this happens, go through your list of goals and re-set any that need revising. When you find yourself questioning your direction, take out your list of goals and go through them. Are those still your objectives? If not, adjust them to reflect the course you wish to take.

d. OUTCOME GOALS

Outcome goals are the events that need to occur to make your adoption happen. They include long-term goals, interim goals, and short-term goals.

Long-term goals involve a series of steps taken over a period of time. These might include gathering information, exploring personal options, choosing the kind of child you wish to parent, selecting a route to adoption, identifying and placing your child in your home, and finalizing the adoption. You may word your long-term goals any way you wish. They should simply sum up a particular stage of adoption which requires a period of time and a number of steps to accomplish.

Long-term goals can be subdivided into interim goals. Gathering information could include, among other things, reading about adoption, joining an adoptive parent group, and talking to friends and family who have experienced adoption. Exploring personal options could be broken down into calling adoption agencies and services in your area, finding out which lawyers do adoptions in your community, speaking to some of them, and calling your public agency and asking them to send you brochures on foster care and adoption.

Short-term goals are the short incremental steps you have to take to realize long-term and interim goals. Where your long-term goal is gathering information and your interim goal under that heading is reading about adoption, your short-term goals might include going to the library and looking up adoption in the catalogue, borrowing or ordering books through an interlibrary loan, searching your library's periodical index for recent magazine articles about adoption, visiting bookstores, contacting an adoptive parent group to find out if they have a library you can borrow from, subscribing to Ours, ordering an adoption catalogue, and calling an adoption agency and asking if they can recommend any books on adoption.

Exercise #3 will help you determine your outcome goals.

EXERCISE #3
SETTING YOUR OUTCOME GOALS

Make a list of everything you need to do to accomplish your adoption. Write down your ideas in any order they occur to you. It's fine to be general at this stage.

Next, take your list and reframe it in terms of goals to be accomplished. Subdivide them into long-term, interim, and short-term goals; you can tailor your approach to whatever format works best for you. Be as elaborate or as simple as you like. You could type or draw blank chart forms and photocopy them to fill in later, or write everything down by hand, or put it on your computer. Whatever your approach, leave room to change or amend your list, and reframe your goals. The important thing now is to get something in writing.

There are several purposes to this exercise:

(a) To take control of your adoption

(b) To help you plan how to allocate your time and energy effectively

(c) To create a "tickler" list to remind you of tasks to do and any deadlines you'll have to meet

(d) To provide a framework for adoption recordkeeping

(e) To create a permanent record for your child

e. PROCESS GOALS

How you go about achieving your goals is often as important as the final outcome. Some families, consciously or unwittingly, use an illegal or unethical route to adoption. It is easy to become so focused on the final outcome that we pay too little attention to how we arrive at our destination and what that means of transportation means for us and our children.

If you have doubts about anything you are asked to do to accomplish your adoption, use this rule of thumb. Ask yourself how you will explain it to your child in 20 years. How will your child feel about hearing the steps you took to accomplish the adoption? Early on in our adoption experience, my husband and I decided that we wanted an adoption that had come about as a result of a birth family's decision made before they knew about our family. We asked our lawyer to find us a child who was already in foster care or an orphanage before we were introduced as prospective adopters. This is by no means the only or the best way to approach adoption. But it was the process that we felt most comfortable with. Take some time to think about the way you want your child to come to you.

You might set process goals for the following:

(a) The way you learn about adoption

(b) How you keep abreast of changes that could affect your adoption experience

(c) How you organize your adoption records (there will be a lot of them)

(d) How you maintain a sense of control over your adoption

(e) How you find support and cope with the emotional ups and downs

(f) How you verify that sources and adoption professionals are qualified and ethical professionals

Exercise #4 will help you focus on your process goals and Checklist #1 is an example of how to record your goals.

EXERCISE #4
SETTING YOUR PROCESS GOALS

Create process goals for yourself. How do you want to accomplish your adoption? How do you plan to keep your emotional equilibrium? What steps can you take to protect your personal relationships from being hurt by the stresses of adoption? How much time each week are you prepared to put into your adoption and how will you keep track?

Each month, write down your goals and divide them into individual tasks. For example, you might set the goal of keeping your records organized, and assign yourself the tasks of creating and updating an indexing system, adding names of adoption resource people to your rolodex, and reviewing your adoption documents every week.

As you start your adoption you may not have many process goals. But as you move through your adoption there will be fewer outcome goals to take care of and more process goals as the tension builds.

Sooner or later, adopters get to the point where all you can do is wait. Keeping your sanity and at the same time planning optimistically for the time when you'll bring your child home can be tricky. When you find that there is no work left to do on the adoption itself and yet nothing seems to be happening, set some post-adoption goals. Especially for those who are currently childless, time to yourselves will soon be only a remembered luxury. Now is the time to read child development books, rent a video on Honduras, and take a relaxing vacation with your significant other.

CHECKLIST #1
SETTING GOALS

EXAMPLE OF OUTCOME GOAL WORKSHEET		
LONG–TERM GOAL: gathering information **INTERIM GOAL**: reading about adoption		
SHORT–TERM GOAL: Task to be accomplished	Done	Comments
VISIT THE LIBRARY	√	
Check the periodical index	√	
Read news articles about adoption	√	
Look up adoption in professional social work journals	√	photocopied 2 articles
Do a book search on the library computer	√	
Order books through interlibrary loan		ordered *International* *Adoption*
Check out adoption books	√	brought 3 books home to read
SUBSCRIBE TO ADOPTION PERIODICALS	√	
Ours	√	(date)
Roots and wings	√	(date)
local adoption support group newsletter	√	(date)
CALL LOCAL ADOPTION SUPPORT GROUP	√	left message on answering machine
Ask if I can borrow adoption directories	√	(date)

EXAMPLE OF PROCESS GOAL WORKSHEET		
PROCESS GOAL: Recordkeeping for the month of January		
TASK TO BE ACCOMPLISHED	Done	Comments
Create and update indexing system	√	labeled accordian file folder
Add names of adoption resource people to rolodex weekly	√	
Go through adoption documents weekly and file	√	
Review goal lists once a week	√	
PROCESS GOAL: Maintaining emotional balance for the month of January		
TASK TO BE ACCOMPLISHED	Done	Comments
Maintain weekly contact with adoption buddy	√	Lunch (date); called 3 times
Go out to dinner with partner once a week and promise not to talk about adoption!	√	
Investigate support groups	√	Joined local waiting parent group
Attend yoga classes each week	√	
Plan a vacation	√	Called travel agent about 1 week trip to Mexico

1. Becoming and staying informed

How often will you read about adoption? Will you set aside a period of time each week to research adoption issues? How many agencies will you call or write to per week? Will you set money aside to spend on becoming informed? How much? Writing down all your adoption-related questions before talking or writing to agency officials is a process goal.

Early on, if you are a couple, you need to consider how you will divide adoption-related tasks. Often, it is the woman who enables the adoption, does the reading, makes all or most calls and takes the initiative in decision-making. This gives her more power and responsibility than her partner. If the wife is at home while the husband is working at a job, it may make sense for her to make phone calls and take care of some adoption business. However, it is important for both partners to take responsibility for the adoption. Some tasks are emotionally draining and need to be shared. Both partners need to be fully involved in important decisions.

How will you update your information? What steps will you take to ensure that information you receive is accurate? Regular attendance at an adoption support group is one way. You might decide to check your library's periodical index at set intervals. If you are working with an agency, how often will you call them for an update on your case? What questions will you ask when you do?

2. Keeping track

No matter what kind of adoption you pursue, it will generate reams of paper, telephone numbers and messages, vital documents, and records. To the extent that you are well organized, you can save hours of frantic searching. I recommend that you set up a tracking system and evaluate it periodically. Accordion file folders with labeled pockets are useful. From the beginning, figure out how and where you will keep your adoption records. Whenever you need to obtain an important document such as a birth certificate, order at least three copies.

If you find yourself abandoning one adoption route and picking up another, it is more than likely that you will have to assemble a completely new set of documents for the second adoption.

A rolodex of adoption-related phone numbers may be helpful. Keep a copy of all correspondence. Photocopy or print out an extra computer copy of every letter you send and keep all letters sent to you. Make a note of the date, who you spoke to, and a summary of what was said in every conversation you have with an adoption professional about your adoption.

3. Empowerment

How can you take charge of your adoption? Reading up on a subject and formulating and writing down your questions before you speak to an adoption professional can be empowering. When the person you are speaking to senses that you have concrete goals and are focused on them, you are more likely to get concrete answers to your questions than if you are vague, hesitant, and don't seem to know exactly what you are seeking.

If you are single, it may help to bring a close friend or relative along to a meeting at an agency. Finding an agency that will allow you to have a friend present at your home study also might be empowering. Consider what other steps you can take to feel in control.

4. Finding and maintaining a support network

We all need emotional support at times. However, no single approach is best for everyone. Some do well in formal support groups. Others prefer to rely on an informal network of family and friends. For those who live in rural areas, the challenge may be putting together a local network of support.

Some need more support than others. Preferential adopters who already have biological children and are confident in their role as parents may need less support than a childless couple emerging from years of unsuccessful infertility treatment. Experienced parents may focus more on the formal adoption process, while infertile adopters may seek support and education in parenting issues.

Consider what kind of support works best for you. How will you go about getting it? What areas do you need support in? If you live in a rural area, you might explore a computer network for support or write to an adoption magazine and ask for pen pals who have experienced what you're going through. You might pick a close friend to confide in. A friend and I became adoption "buddies." We came to the decision to adopt at the same time and shared the work, the joys, and the pain of adoption every step of the way. We set time aside to call up adoption agencies and together formulated questions to ask them. We lent each other books and passed on information, shared sources, vented our frustrations with the slowness of the process, and were there for each other whenever necessary. In the end, our adoptions became so intertwined that two of our children were fostered by the same Brazilian family.

If you enjoy a group setting, an adoption support group is a great resource. If you come out of the experience of infertility you can draw on resources such as RESOLVE to find a support network. A group can brainstorm together and help one another meet their adoption goals. Some have even found their child this way.

Whichever route you choose to find support, make sure you have it! Adoption can be a lonely experience. As David Kirk notes in his book *Shared Fate*, adopters face subtle discrimination from society at large. You are certain to encounter insensitive remarks and people who question your choices. When you experience a devastating setback — the child you had begun to think of as yours is not free for adoption after all, or the country you were counting on adopting from suddenly bans international adoption — no one will understand as well as another adoptive parent.

If you are a couple, you may be inclined to rely only on one another for all support. That is usually a poor idea. After a setback you may both be depressed and unable to lift one another's spirits. You will be putting a strain on your relationship, too, since you will be asking the other person to meet your emotional needs at exactly the time when your partner's needs are greatest.

5. Dealing with emotional highs and lows

Most adoptions are roller coaster rides. There are long straight stretches, sudden lurches upward, and swooping plunges to the ground. There are people for whom an adoption seems to go like clockwork, but they are in the minority. Even an adoption that seems like a sure thing may suddenly fall apart. Because there are many areas over which you have no control, you cannot plan your way to a certain result. By setting and maintaining goals, you can ensure that you take advantage of opportunities to control your experience to the greatest extent possible. But how will you handle the inevitable twists of fate?

Making a plan for how you will respond to good or bad news can help. Adoption lawyers say that they spend a lot of office time with clients either persuading them not to be carried away by euphoria over a good prospect or encouraging them to try again when a prospect falls through. What is your own emotional style? Do you go to extremes? Do you let out your feelings easily or are you somewhat reserved or even repressed? If you are a couple, how do your styles work together? Maybe one of you is better suited to making follow-up calls to an agency, while the other is happier doing research in a library. (If you are single, it may help to identify someone who is willing to be there for you any time, day or night, someone you can call with good news or bad.)

If you find yourself becoming anxious will you seek counseling? What has worked for you in the past in getting over emotional hurdles? Can you adapt a successful technique to your adoption in advance? Massage therapy or exercise may help. If you are experiencing a long wait, don't put the rest of your life on hold. Taking vacations and engaging in activities that bring you pleasure are important in maintaining your emotional balance. Chapter 12 offers more suggestions for coping with the wait for a child.

RESOURCE GUIDE

Bransford, John D. and Barry S. Stein. *The Ideal Problem Solver: A Guide for Improved Thinking, Learning, and Creativity.* New York: W.H. Freeman and Company, 1984.

Lynch, Richard. *Getting Out of Your Own Way.* Seattle, WA: Abbott Press, 1989.

McKay, Matthew, Martha Davis, and Patrick Fanning. *Messages: The Communication Book.* Oakland, CA: New Harbinger Publications, 1983.

Robbins, Anthony. *Awaken the Giant Within: How to Take Immediate Control of Your Mental, Emotional, Physical, and Financial Destiny.* New York: Simon & Schuster, 1991.

Wheeler, David D. and Irving L. Janis. *A Practical Guide for Making Decisions.* New York: Free Press, 1980.

TIPS

When you are setting adoption goals, and throughout the adoption process, look for resources outside the field of infertility and adoption. Books on business theory offer suggestions on goal setting, time management, interviewing, and evaluation. Self-help books give suggestions on coping with stress and emotional upheaval. Writers on meditation, creative visualization, and philosophy may all have something useful to contribute.

7
AGENCY ADOPTION

a. A CONSUMER'S LOOK AT ADOPTION AGENCIES

There are hundreds of licensed adoption agencies in the United States. Every year new ones open and others go out of business. While licensers try to keep track of them, they do not always have the resources to monitor agency activities closely. Most agencies do operate ethically. Often understaffed and overworked, they manage to provide valuable, high quality services to children, adopters, and birth parents. But some do not have such high standards and since no agency hangs up a sign saying "We offer slipshod service," adopters must learn how to make this determination for themselves. As consumers, we need to take time to evaluate carefully any agency we consider working with.

This chapter focuses on private agencies. Because public agencies are a part of state government, they are subject to the laws and regulations governing state agency practices. Their operations are under constant supervision and while that doesn't guarantee they will operate perfectly all the time, they are as accountable as any other arm of state government. Adopters can use the tools available to any consumer of public services in dealing with public adoption agencies.

Consumers need to be especially wary when evaluating an agency engaging in international adoption. International programs offered by agencies currently receive limited regulatory oversight, although this should change when the Hague Convention is implemented. There are exceptions: in some countries, international adoption is closely scrutinized by the local government and permission to place children in the United States and Canada is limited to a few agencies, which are carefully screened.

Some agencies in the United States have operated excellent international programs for years. Many are scrupulously honest, well-informed, and take care to follow the laws of any jurisdiction they may be operating in. Problems more often arise with new, inexperienced agencies with little or no track record in the country or in international adoption. Such agencies may have little knowledge of the laws of the country they are placing from, and may rely on intermediaries whose credentials and honesty they have not evaluated.

Some agencies are well-intentioned, but incompetent. Because these agencies are located in the United States, but their international activities take place abroad, it is difficult for state licensing authorities to follow them. The agency and its agents in the program country may not be subject to regulations.

If no one in a U.S. agency speaks the language of the country they place from and if they rely on an intermediary whose qualifications they have no means of verifying, they may unwittingly support fraudulent or illegal practices. Some U.S. agencies fail to realize that huge adoption fees charged by the intermediaries they work with in developing countries may provide great incentive to bend or break the law — some of those fees themselves may be against the law. An agency may be no more knowledgeable than adoptive families about what constitutes a valid adoption in another country. It is up to adoptive parents to verify agency competence and ethics before committing to an international adoption. If we don't, our children and their birth families will pay the price.

1. The licensing process

All private U.S. adoption agencies are regulated by their state government and must meet certain basic standards to receive a license to operate. These standards vary from state to state. The licensing authority reviews the applicant's financial affairs, the services they plan to offer, and the qualifications of the staff to deliver them. However, the investigation may be quite limited depending on the licenser's budget. There are reports of agencies being given a license in one state after having a license revoked for misconduct in another state.

Few, if any, agencies are regulated closely after licensing. State governments lack resources for such monitoring, and unless a complaint is received about an agency, its practices are unlikely to be scrutinized. Although agencies must apply for relicensing about once every three years, the process is virtually automatic in the absence of complaints. Some, but not all, states require a periodic financial audit of agencies. In order for the overall standard of agency practice to rise, adopters must be willing to play our essential role as responsible service consumers. That means evaluating the services received and giving useful feedback to agencies and regulators whether service quality is high or unacceptably low.

The reluctance of adopters to complain about poor agency service arises from several factors. One is the fear that by making a complaint, adopters will be "blackballed" and lose the opportunity to adopt at all. Because adopters have no right to a child per se, it is hard to take a step that could jeopardize their fragile position. This has led to a situation in which agencies that have provided poor service and even broken laws, continue to operate unhindered.

The state adoption specialist and licensing authority are essential resources for adopters. They will listen to any complaint you have about any adoption agency or service in your state. This doesn't mean that every complaint is founded in agency misconduct. Some adopter complaints arise from a misunderstanding of legitimate agency practice or communication problems with agency personnel. But if after attempting to resolve the problem with the agency you are still unsatisfied, you may get to the bottom of the problem more quickly by contacting the licensing authority and discussing the issue. Payment problems, suspicion of illegality, or racial discrimination on the part of agency staff are examples of issues that should be brought to the attention of the state adoption authorities.

One little known fact about adoption licensing authorities is that they can investigate interstate and international adoption problems if it involves an agency that is licensed in their state. Even though a U.S. state government has no authority over another country's laws, it can investigate whether a placement facilitated by a state-licensed agency complies with U.S. and state laws and the charter of the agency involved. Licensers of different states are in contact with each other and share information and concerns.

2. Consumer evaluation

What can adopters learn from evaluating an agency? Let's use adoption fees as an example. High fees do not necessarily correspond to better service. In fact, if they are too high they may signal an illegal or unethical adoption.

If you research current fees for an adoption service, you will be able to evaluate whether an agency's fee is above or below the norm. If an agency you are considering charges a fee 150% higher than other agencies in your state, you can choose to go to a less expensive agency, decide to pay the fee anyway, or ask the agency to explain the discrepancy. Too many adopters choose the first two options without discussing the discrepancy with the agency or anyone else. But if you ask them to explain their fee structure, you will receive an answer that can give you important information. Perhaps the fee is higher because more services are provided. Perhaps the agency is supporting an orphanage in Latin America or subsidizing adoption fees for adopters with low incomes. Perhaps the fee is higher because the agency is a for-profit business and is advertising on television and radio to locate

123

birth mothers. Perhaps the fee is higher because illegal payments are being made to birth mothers to persuade them to place their children with that agency. Perhaps no one at the agency knows why their fees are higher, or cares.

Whatever the answer it will provide you with useful information which you can use to compare the agency to other options you are exploring. The willingness of an agency to respond to your questions will tell you how committed they are to providing good service.

3. Accountability

Be polite, professional, and as understanding as possible when dealing with agency personnel. Most agency workers are doing the best job they can under the circumstances. Imagine yourself in the position of agency staff and try to see yourself through their eyes. Is what you are asking really possible? Reasonable? Is it or should it be within their power to accomplish? Give an agency the benefit of the doubt, but recognize that as a paying customer you are entitled to a basic level of service. At a minimum, agencies should:

(a) Be familiar with state law and regulations affecting adoptions, as well as federal laws and those of other countries if they are placing children from those countries

(b) Comply with these laws and regulations and explain them to clients in advance

(c) Be responsive to client concerns and return phone calls

(d) Have a contingency plan for adoptions that fall through. (The plan should include provision for returning, forfeiting or adjusting fees paid, and whether another equivalent option will be offered to the client. Many aspects of adoption — especially international adoption — are wholly beyond agency control. This makes it all the more important that agencies have contingency plans that can be explained to adopters *before* they make a decision or pay a fee.)

(e) Be willing to provide you with several references of families who have used their services within the past year

Responsible agencies are glad to explain their practices and answer questions from interested adopters. It saves them valuable time, avoids communication problems, and shows that adopters care about how children come to them. A list of questions to ask is provided in this chapter to help you evaluate different agency adoption services.

If you have reason to believe that an agency has acted unethically, illegally, or negligently, and after following the steps described above you are still unable to resolve the problem satisfactorily, it is important to pass this information on. If after making a report to your state adoption and licensing authority they are unable to resolve the problem, inform adoptive parent groups in your area, AFA, or other national adoption organizations. You can help other adopters avoid the problems you fell into and play a part in raising the standards of adoption practice.

b. HOW TO LOCATE AGENCIES

Finding adoption agencies has never been easier. NAIC lists hundreds in the National Adoption Directory and can conduct a personalized computer search of agencies for you. The International Concerns Committee for Children (ICCC), discussed in chapter 3, publishes a guidebook listing most agencies that place children internationally, some that place children domestically, agencies that place children in Canadian homes, and agencies that serve single adopters.

Several books on adoption list agencies, although their information may not be current. Additional sources are listed in the Resource Guide at the end of this chapter. Support groups for non-traditional adopters publish lists of agencies that accept them as clients. If you are single, gay or lesbian, or older, starting with one of these lists can save you time and energy. See the Resource Guide for chapter 5.

An adoptive parent group or local library may also have adoption directories that you can inspect or check out. You can also call your local public agency and ask if they have any listings you can look at. The bigger the sample of agencies you investigate, the more accurate the picture you will form of the existing alternatives.

c. HOW TO EVALUATE AN AGENCY

Before you interview an agency, ask them to send you any materials they have about their programs. Most have written guidelines describing services, eligibility criteria, and fees. Some are detailed and will answer many questions; others are brief fact sheets. Look for clues about the agency in what they send you. Do they send a brochure with fees for the current year and a summary of programs and guidelines? Or are the materials photocopies of photocopies filled with typos and grammatical errors?

Even the best written guidelines offer limited information. Few agencies discuss in detail where your fees go or how long a waiting period for a child is likely to be. In many cases the answers aren't provided because they will vary from adopter to adopter and the fact sheet was written for all kinds of adopters. Thus, after an agency has provided you with written information you will need to formulate questions to address your own concerns.

Checklist #2 at the end of this chapter contains questions to ask when evaluating an adoption agency. You may think of others. For comparison, ask the same questions of each agency. Put them in writing and make an appointment to discuss them with an agency intake worker, in person or by telephone. If you don't put them in writing, after interviewing several agencies you may have trouble remembering what answer was given by which agency. Note the name of whomever you speak to.

An agency that is not willing to take the time to go through this process with you may not take time to address your concerns later, either. The way an agency responds to requests for information from prospective clients will reveal the level of their commitment to client service.

You also should interview other adopters who have used the same agency you are considering. Most adoptive parent groups keep records of where their members adopted and through what source. They may be able to tell you if a member had a bad experience with an agency. Ask adopters if they would use the agency they adopted from again and why. Remember that some adopters are nervous about sharing negative information with strangers. You should be prepared to offer and honor confidentiality. However if you hear something that suggests that an adoption agency is breaking the law or operating in an unethical manner, you may wish to draw this fact to the attention of the group's leadership and urge the adopter to consider making a formal complaint.

d. FOR-PROFIT AGENCIES

Adoption agencies operating as for-profit businesses have opened in many states. They are subject to the same licensing guidelines as private non-profit agencies. However, they are allowed to earn a profit and are not subject to the laws governing the operation of a non-profit corporation. Many of the non-profit agencies, because they have tax-exempt status, obtain federal, state, and private grants and donations to help offset operating costs and to support services. For-profit agencies must finance their operations out of the fees charged to clients, which can make them relatively risky as a business proposition. Some do go out of business quickly, leaving behind adopter clients who have paid large fees for nothing in return.

However, although some for-profit agencies have had a short, unhappy life span, others have thrived over a period of years. These often succeed because they offer valuable services to birth parents above and beyond what is available elsewhere. They may be more flexible in eligibility criteria for adopters, in arranging open adoptions, or in reaching birth mothers. However, the pressures on them are also great. Any adopter considering working with a for-profit agency needs to weigh the pros and cons carefully. What does this agency offer that a non-profit does not? Compare answers to questions on the checklist. Do they make more successful placements? Are adopters happier? Are birth parents? Do they have a track record of years?

Some for-profit agencies place internationally born children. In that case, you need to be especially careful because regulation of the agency is likely to be limited. Working with a licensed adoption agency or government department in another country is one indication that the agency is considered respectable. I recommend that you seek information about any for-profit agency placing internationally from a highly reputable source before working with it. See the Resource Guide in chapter 3 for further suggestions.

Compare the for-profit agency's fees with those of non-profit agencies and facilitators. If the agency is making promises that no other agency makes with respect to children of the country involved, this may signal irregularities and illegalities in the placement process. A legal adoption in most countries takes time. It is unlikely that a baby will be free for adoption before two or three months of age. A guarantee of race is suspect. Be especially wary of agencies that promise the adoption will be completed within a brief, exact period of time. A legal adoption will almost certainly be subject to factors beyond the agency's control.

e. WORKING WITH AN AGENCY OVER TIME

Once you have decided you wish to work with an agency, you are embarking on an intense relationship that may last for years. As with any relationship, it works best when you make your expectations clear, communicate honestly and directly with each other, and raise and resolve concerns and conflicts as they arise.

Knowing what you want is important from the time you first fill out an agency's intake application. The form will almost certainly ask you to state what kind of child you are willing to accept. Will you accept only a same-race infant or an older child of a different race? A child with a correctable handicap? A sibling group? Many adopters feel a subtle pressure to say they will accept a wide variety of children, even when they feel passionately that they want as young and healthy a baby as possible.

It is important to be honest about your feelings now. For infertile adopters, the usual preference is for a healthy baby and it needs no apology. It is natural to want to parent the same kind of child you would have had if you weren't infertile. Agency forms, however, are used for all adopters. By listing options other than healthy, same-race infants, an agency is telling you that such children are available; it is not pressuring you to adopt them.

Many adopters have mixed feelings that shift over the course of the adoption process. Tell the agency if you are ambivalent. The clearer you make your feelings to the agency, the better job they will be able to do matching you with a child and helping you build your family. When deciding on the degree of contact you are willing to accept with birth parents, be equally honest.

The home study process is often the most intense contact adopters have with agency personnel. The process may feel humiliating at times, highlighting the differences between

129

adoption and biological parenting. Adopters are torn — you want to be honest but you also want to appear in the best light as parent material.

Good agency workers are aware of and sensitive to adopter feelings about the home study. Within the adoption community, many professionals are seeking ways to make the process more humane and less judgmental. Some agencies are doing group home studies for several families at once. Others have renamed the process something like "adoption planning" and focus on helping adopters acquire the skills to adopt and parent successfully. But most adopters still find the process difficult. Because each state requires that an agency home study demonstrate parental fitness in order for a legal adoption to take place, no matter what it is called, it is still a "test" of adopters. Choosing an agency that actively seeks to make the home study a positive experience can help. Being honest with case workers about your feelings may also help.

When you are unhappy with your agency, your first response should be to tell them. Discuss the problem with your case worker. If the discussion doesn't lead to an improvement, approach the case worker's supervisor. In many cases that will take you to the top of the agency hierarchy. Adoption is an institution which works only if all parties are satisfied. Unlike biological parents, adopters are choosing much of their parenting experience. Take advantage of this difference and express your preferences and views candidly. At the same time, recognize that there are variables beyond anyone's control and that risks exist along the spectrum from beginning to end. Your "healthy" newborn may prove to have fetal alcohol effects. More than one birth mother may change her mind. This happens even in the best agencies. Hold the agency responsible only for what it has or should have control over.

Finally, there is no substitute for someone who has been there. In dealing with the stresses of adoption, the best agency will sometimes seem more of a hindrance to adopting than a help. Don't rely on your case worker for moral support. Other adoptive parents are often the only ones who can truly understand: friends who have adopted, adoptive parent groups, adoption newsletters. When you have finally completed your adoption, consider offering your services as a volunteer to your agency to give such information and support to other adoptive parents.

f. RECORDKEEPING FOR AN AGENCY ADOPTION

Recordkeeping is easier in an agency than an independent adoption. Your case worker will keep a file on your adoption and the agency will let you know what documents you need and may help you to obtain them. I recommend that you also keep a parallel file on your adoption including each document you provide to the agency (an original, if possible), a record of each telephone contact you have with the agency, receipts for all payments related to the adoption, and any notes you may have made about the agency, or received from other adopters.

Many adopters change agencies and approaches during the adoption process. If you obtain and hold onto originals of all your documents, you will be well positioned to start over, if necessary. You will also have a record of your communication with and payments to the agency if they are needed to make a complaint or resolve a dispute. In addition, the receipts can be produced if you are eligible for an adoption subsidy or if adoptions become tax-deductible. (The adoption community has lobbied for years to make some or all adoption expenses tax-deductible and has come increasingly close to succeeding. If and when this occurs, adopters will need a record of all payments made towards their adoption.) Most important, keeping a complete adoption file will help you to feel in charge of your adoption. And when you come to prepare your child's life book, the adoption file is a ready-made piece of your family history.

g. POST-PLACEMENT

1. Post-placement studies

Like the home study, a post-placement study usually involves several meetings with your case worker, at least one of which is in your home. The objective is to verify that the placement is successful. The worker will then make a written recommendation to the court that the adoption be finalized. In some states, home studies and post-placement studies are done together, since children are allowed to be placed in a home before a home study has been carried out. In some states, no home study is required for relative and stepparent adoptions, but a post-placement study is done.

Information about the child's schedule, any adjustment difficulties, and how everyone is feeling about the adoption is sought. If adopters are having problems, now is the time to say so and seek help. A good agency can help you find community resources to resolve adjustment problems. Generally, the post-placement study is straightforward, but in a special needs adoption, it is more significant. Identifying underlying health or emotional issues now can help adopters obtain substantial financial benefits to address them. After finalization, these benefits may not be available.

In very rare cases, a case worker may recommend against adoption. Before such a step is taken, case workers bring their concerns to the attention of adopters who are given the opportunity to correct it. Options for dealing with a recommendation against adoption include seeking a post-placement study from another source or petitioning the court to approve the adoption anyway. If the agency is the child's legal guardian, they have the option of removing the child from the home of the adopters.

2. Finalization

After you have accepted the referral and the child is placed in your home, the last step is to finalize the adoption in court.

The agency, usually through its attorney, will take care of the paperwork, set a date for a court hearing, and guide you through the process. At that time the adoption petition will be presented to the judge who will verify that the adoption is lawful and in the child's best interests. The hearing may be in a private courtroom (since all adoption proceedings are confidential) or in the judge's chambers. In addition to the adoptive family, the agency case worker who did the home study and post placement study will generally be present. The process is straightforward. In addition to reviewing the documents, the judge may ask questions of the case worker, the adoptive family, and the adoptee, if the child is old enough.

It is natural for adopters to be a little tense and anxious going to court. The hearing marks the end of a long and difficult journey. What if something goes wrong now? In fact, the occasion is usually a very happy one. Judges enjoy adoptions. Most of their work involves resolving disputes and trying and sentencing criminal offenders. Creating a new family may be the high point of their week.

Many are happy to pose with the child and parents for a photo. However, some draw the line at videotaping. Since the proceedings are supposed to be confidential, the sight of a video camera makes judges nervous. If you would like to tape some of the proceedings, you should contact the court prior to the hearing and seek advance permission.

CHECKLIST #2
QUESTIONS TO ASK ADOPTION AGENCIES

a. GENERAL

Not all of these questions can be answered precisely. There are many variables in adoption and to a question like "How long will we have to wait for a child" you will get—at best—a very general response. Beware the "too good to be true" syndrome. As with everything else in life, if it sounds too good to be true, it almost certainly is.

1. Who can adopt? (Always ask this first. If you don't meet their eligibility criteria, there's no point in asking anything else.)

2. Who is your client? (The child to be placed, the adopter, the whole adoption triad? No answer is right or wrong, but it will reveal the agency's adoption philosophy.)

3. Describe the children you place.

4. Describe the services and programs you provide.

5. How do children come to be available through your agency? (Do they work cooperatively with a public agency, birth parents, out of state affiliates, attorneys?)

6. How long has your agency been in operation?

7. How many children have you placed in each of the last three years?

8. How many children have you placed in each of the past three years in families similar to ours? (In age, marital status, religion, sexual orientation, children already in the family.)

9. What are your fees? (Ask for a breakdown by services such as intake application fees, home study, home study updates, pre-placement processing, placement fees, services to birth parents, legal fees, post-placement study, and finalization.)

For each fee ask:

- What will my fee be paying for? (An intake application fee may cover the cost of mailing you the form or be applied to agency overhead.)

- Is any fee refundable? If not, why not? If it is partly refundable, when and how can a refund be obtained?

- Can fees change without notice? If I have already paid the fee and it is revised upward, must I pay more?

- When did your agency last raise its fees? By how much? Why?

- When and how must fees be paid? Can they be amortized (spread out over time, such as in monthly installments)?

- Where fees are variable, what is the most adopters have paid? The least? What were the circumstances? (Note: If your resources are limited, you should budget for the most expensive scenario. Ask yourself whether you will have sufficient funds left over, after paying, to try again if the adoption doesn't work out.)

10. Once I enter a program, can I transfer to another one easily? (such as moving from domestic to international adoption)

11. Do you work with a public agency or adoption exchange? (An affirmative answer means a state agency has contracted with them to help find homes for children and sees them as a responsible service provider.)

12. What education and experience do your case workers have? Do they have degrees in social work or counseling? How many years of experience in adoption? What is the case load like? Do you have a high staff turnover?

13. Once we submit an application, how long must we wait until we receive a home study?

14. What does a home study with your agency entail? (such as a financial statement, written adopter autobiography, references, doctor's letter, psychological evaluation, criminal background check, employment verification, insurance verification)

15. Will you accept a home study done by another agency or service? If not, will you update that home study for a reduced fee or must I go through the entire process over again?

16. If we decide to work with a different source or agency after you have completed our home study, may we use the home study you prepared? If not, why not?

17. Do you have affiliates in other states?

18. Are you affiliated with a religion or particular church? Which one? How (if at all) does this affect an adoption done by your agency (i.e., are most birth parents drawn from this church and is preference given to adopters who are church members)?

19. If, after doing our home study, you do not recommend us, will you tell us why? Can we obtain a copy of our home study? Do you have an appeal or review process in place for adopters who receive a negative home study from a case worker in your agency? How often have you recommended against an adoptive family? For what reasons?

20. Can I join a waiting list for a child before my home study is done or must I wait until after it has been completed?

21. What is the average wait for the referral of a child after adopters join a waiting list? What is the average time a family like us waits for the kind of child we are seeking?

22. Can we specify the age and gender of the child we wish to parent?

23. What happens if we turn down a referral?

24. Do you place transculturally/transracially? Why?

25. (For families who are members of a racial/cultural minority.) Have you had any experience with our group as adopters? Agency rudeness and delays in making referrals have been reported by some minorities. Finding an agency specializing in minority adoption may make your adoption a faster, more positive experience. If you are non-traditional adopters, ask if the agency has ever placed a child in a home similar to yours before. What experience and knowledge of your group do they have?)

26. Does your agency offer services such as classes or support groups for waiting parents?

27. Has your agency ever been involved in a lawsuit? Why? Was it satisfactorily resolved? Is there any current or pending litigation involving your agency?

28. What is involved in the post-placement study? How long does it take?

29. Describe any services you provide to adoptive families between placement and finalization.

30. What happens if problems arise between placement and finalization of the adoption (i.e., if the child has an unforeseen health problem or disability)? Has this ever occurred before in your agency? If so, please describe.

31. After the adoption is finalized, do you continue to provide any services to adoptive families? Which ones and under what circumstances (i.e., ongoing support group for adoptive families, help in obtaining medical assessment)?

32. If we want to adopt a second child in the future, will we be able to do so through this program? A third child? Must we wait a certain period of time before we can seek a new referral? If we adopted through you once, will we receive preference for a future adoption? (Some agencies will place only with childless adopters.)

33. Can you refer me to three families who adopted through your agency in the past year to whom I can talk about their experience? (The agency may need to obtain permission from these families first.)

b. FOR DOMESTIC INFANT ADOPTION

1. How many infant placements have you made in each of the last three years? (The number will be fairly small.)

2. How do you locate birth parents prior to the birth of the child? How are they screened? Do you monitor their health and any risk behaviors during pregnancy? How?

3. Describe all services you offer to birth parents. (Ask for details. "Counseling" can mean a half-hour discussion with a case worker or regular counseling sessions for months before and after childbirth.) Is counseling mandatory or optional?

4. Do birth parents receive separate legal advice?

5. What is the range of openness or confidentiality available through your agency? Do adopters and birth parents have a say or is it determined solely by the agency?

6. What happens if the birth parents we are working with change their minds? (Beware an agency that says this "never happens." Birth parents often do change their minds and an agency that is not open about this fact may be withholding other important information as well.)

7. What happens to money we have paid on behalf of a birth mother who later changes her mind? (It may be non-refundable.)

8. Will we receive priority for a subsequent referral if an adoption plan falls through?

9. In an adoption plan made prior to the birth of the child, what are our options if, after birth, the infant is not what we expected?

10. What is your procedure where the birth father can't be identified or located? (Since much adoption litigation involves birth fathers' rights, a good agency is very careful to obtain proper consents.)

11. Can you refer me to three families who have adopted an infant through your agency in the past two years?

c. **FOR INTERNATIONAL INFANT ADOPTIONS**

1. Which countries do you have programs for?

   For each program you are interested in:

   - How long has this program been in existence?

   - Is the country politically stable? Has it recently undergone a change in government, legal system, or adoption laws? Describe.

   - Has the number of referrals through this country been relatively stable during the course of the program? If not, why not?

   - Does the agency rely on private facilitators or does it work through orphanages and/or state agencies to locate children?

- If the former, what steps do you take to be sure that the facilitator is working within the law of the country?

- Do you have a copy of and/or know the contents of the relevant laws governing adoption in this country?

2. Which services are covered by your fee and which will I be expected to provide and pay for additionally? (such as document translation, foster care, travel arrangements)

3. Can I join two or more programs at once? If not, can you tell me how waiting times compare for each?

4. If a country closes its doors to international adoption before we complete an adoption there, what happens? Do you transfer us to another program automatically or on request? Do we go to the top of another waiting list or do we go to the bottom? What happens to fees we have paid?

5. Do you provide any post-adoption support for international adoptions? (Some agencies sponsor summer culture camps for children, support groups for families who have adopted from a particular country, and volunteer activities to support children's services there.)

6. Can you refer me to three families who have adopted an infant internationally through your agency in the past year? (If you know which program country you are interested in, seek references from adopters who adopted from that program.)

d. FOR SPECIAL NEEDS DOMESTIC ADOPTIONS

1. How do special needs children come to you? Are they all legally free for adoption? (Sometimes children are available because a prior adoption, not necessarily special needs, has disrupted.)

2. Does your agency have a foster adopt or permanency planning program? Please describe.

3. Do you offer services to help our family identify the kind of child we can successful parent? Please describe.

4. Do you offer training or parenting classes to prospective adopters?

5. Do you sponsor peer support groups for parents?

6. Can you help us identify and obtain any financial aid available to us before and after placement and finalization?

7. What services do you offer to adoptive families between referral and finalization? After finalization? If no services are offered, why not? Will you help us locate services we need which you do not provide?

8. Have any special needs adoptions through your agency disrupted in the past three years? Why? What steps does your agency take to prevent adoption disruption?

9. Do you provide any services directly to special needs adoptees? When and under what circumstances?

10. Do you offer respite care for adopters or help them find it?

11. Can you give me three references of families who have adopted special needs children with your help in the past year?

e. FOR SPECIAL NEEDS INTERNATIONAL ADOPTION

1. How do you define special needs? (Some children have correctable medical conditions such as clubfoot or harelip. Others have conditions that may be improved with medical attention, such as spina bifida.)

2. How do special needs children become available to you? (Some agencies work in partnership with orphanages.) Who decided the child had special needs?

3. Can you help us identify the kind of child we can successfully parent?

4. Since it is unlikely that the child will be eligible for an adoption subsidy, can you help us identify medical, social,and educational resources available to us in our community? Can you help us evaluate whether we have the financial means to parent such a child?

5. What information can you give me about the child before I make a decision? (Sometimes photos and videos are available, along with detailed medical assessments. Or there may be only a vague description written by an orphanage worker. In such a case the child may have greater or fewer needs than originally thought.)

CHECKLIST #2 — Continued

6. Have any such adoptions disrupted in the past three years? Why and how? What happens to the child if an adoption disrupts?

7. Can you refer me to three families who have adopted special needs children internationally with your help recently?

RESOURCE GUIDE

1. Adoption agency guides

There are several comprehensive guides to U.S. adoption agencies. Because there are so many agencies, these books are big and often expensive. If your public library or adoptive parent group doesn't have one, you could ask another adopter to split the cost of buying and sharing a book or two with you. If you live in a small community, you may be able to order a directory through an interlibrary loan.

AFA. *Adoption Resources and Information.*

    (To obtain a free copy, write to AFA at the address listed in the chapter 1 Resource Guide.)

ICCC Handbook. (See listing in chapter 3 Resource Guide.)

National Adoption Information Clearinghouse. *National Adoption Directory.* Rockville, MD: NAIC, annual.

    (To obtain the directory, contact NAIC at the address listed in the chapter 1 Resource Guide.)

Posner, Julia. *Adoption Resource Guide: CWLA's Guide to Adoption Agencies: A National Directory of Adoption Agencies & Adoption Resources.* Washington, D.C.: Child Welfare League of America, 1989.

Walker, Elaine L. *Loving Journeys: Guide to Adoption.* Peterborough, NH: Loving Journeys, 1992.

TIPS

While any one of these guides may seem very complete, never consult just one. Most guidebook writers publish only the information that agencies send them. If an agency does not respond to a request for information, it will not be included. Often an agency will respond, but not to all questions. Not all these guides contain the same information about the agencies they survey. Most include details of agency eligibility criteria, number of placements, and sources of children. *Loving Journeys* includes licensed facilitators, adoption attorneys, whether agencies are non- or for-profit, and whether they place with gays and lesbians. The NAIC guidebook has the biggest listing, but does not include information about agency policies.

    Just because an agency doesn't appear in a directory or provide complete information is no reason to assume that it is operating illegally or unethically. The guidebook editor may have missed them when they sent out questionnaires. The agency's response may have been lost in the mail or they may simply have lacked the time and personnel to fill it out and send it to the editor on time. Equally, an agency that looks great in a guidebook listing may be shoddy and unethical in its practices. If you read the small print you'll see that directory compilers do not guarantee the truth of the information agencies send them. They have no way of doing so.

When researching agencies, always consult the most recent directories you can find, and compare listings between different directories. (Some agencies will be listed only in the NAIC Directory.) This way you won't accidentally miss a good prospect because it wasn't in the one directory you looked at.

8
INDEPENDENT ADOPTION

a. A CONSUMER'S LOOK AT ADOPTION FACILITATION SERVICES

Two-thirds of infant adoptions in the United States are carried out independently. International adoptions are often independently contracted. The primary appeal of independent adoption is that it allows adopters to make an adoption plan directly with birth parents and/or their representatives, bypassing agency gatekeepers. Issues such as age, sexual orientation, marital status, and religion are not barriers. Adopters must merely meet their state's legal definition of who may adopt, find birth parents who agree to place a child with them, obtain a home study, and, if everyone is satisfied with the plan after the child's birth, petition a court to approve the adoption. With the exception of the six states discussed in section (e) below, independent adoption is permitted in the U.S. as long as it is carried out lawfully.

The boom in independent adoption has led to the development of sophisticated adoption facilitation services. Today, some are provided through licensed adoption agencies. Others are independent businesses. Adoption attorneys have law practices that are — in essence — facilitation businesses spanning the country. Some independent facilitation services are volunteer operations, staffed by adopters who wish to share their experience with other hopeful parents. Like adoption attorneys, these facilitators are not usually licensed as agencies, since they don't acquire custody of the children, do home studies, or make placement decisions. Facilitators may help adopters locate birth parents and advise them how to present themselves in order to interest birth parents in placing with them. A facilitator may do as little as bringing an adopter to the attention of a pregnant woman or as much as shepherding adopters through the full process and representing them in court.

Today, birth parents are more likely to choose independent adoption because it allows them to exercise more control over who parents their child and the degree of contact with the adoptive family. It allows them to minimize contact with social workers they may perceive as judgmental and intimidating. Birth parents with prior experience of social service bureaucracy may be reluctant to place themselves in agency hands. Unfortunately, this sometimes leads to their being taken advantage of by unscrupulous facilitators whose interest is to provide a newborn baby to adopter clients, not to help birth parents make an important life decision.

When evaluating facilitators, try to compare fees between services which are roughly equivalent. Independent adoption has the most fee variability of all adoptions. If you use a volunteer facilitator, do a lot of the work yourself, and your birth mother has full medical coverage, your entire adoption could cost as little as $2,000. On the other hand, if you use a nationally known attorney, do little work yourself, and pay all medical expenses, if the process of obtaining birth parent consents is complicated, and if the birth mother has a difficult delivery such as a caesarean section, your fee could be $20,000 or more. Some expenses can be anticipated, but you will need to allow for unforeseen contingencies. Adoption insurance might be worth investigating.

In planning an independent adoption, it is important to use an ethical, competent facilitator. You will be responsible for the adoption and your family will have to live with the results. While national adoption advocacy organizations have collected statistics on agencies, no complete compilation of facilitation services has been made. A few books list adoption attorneys, but since many facilitators are part-time businesses or off-shoots of other professions such as law and social work, it may be difficult to identify services for the purpose of comparison.

Although your state licensing authority may not directly regulate a facilitation service, they may be able to tell you if they know of or have received complaints about it. Some facilitators are adoption professionals who worked in adoption agencies first and have a reputation within the adoption community. The agency, usually the attorney general's department responsible for consumer protection, may also have information. And while it's a long shot, don't forget to check with the Better Business Bureau.

Choosing a new, unlicensed facilitation service is risky. If it has no track record, it may be difficult to evaluate. That doesn't mean that the service will be bad, simply that you will have little information to go on.

Facilitation services offered by attorneys are easier to evaluate. Adoption is a legal subspecialty. Lawyers who specialize in adoption or devote a considerable percentage of their practice to it, are usually members of the adoption bar. You can check with your local or state bar association to ascertain the experience of your attorney.

Social workers are also subject to regulation. Check with a professional social work organization, such as the American Council of Social Workers and/or the state adoption specialist. Don't assume that because an adoption facilitator advertises in an adoption periodical such as *Ours*, it is a good source. No adoption periodical has resources to investigate the credentials of its advertisers. While they would not knowingly accept advertising from an illegal facilitator, they have no way to verify that a facilitator is operating legally.

b. LOCATING FACILITATORS

Contact adoption agencies and ask if they facilitate independent adoptions. Some offer programs in which they help adopters locate birth parents, mediate contact issues, and ensure birth parent rights are respected. These services may or may not be more expensive than non-agency facilitation, but they can give you the freedom of independent adoption with less risk.

Some larger independent facilitators are listed in the phone book. Adoptive parent support groups are an excellent source for referrals. Your state bar association can give you names of attorneys who are members of the adoption bar. *Loving Journeys*, listed in the Resource Guide of chapter 7, lists adoption attorneys. Some facilitators place across the country, bringing together birth parents and adopters who may live thousands of miles apart. They often advertise in newspapers or adoptive parent magazines. If your birth mother lives in another state and gives birth there, you will need to obtain Interstate Compact approval. The extra legal work will add to the cost of your adoption.

Before you search for a facilitator, consider how much work you are prepared to do on your adoption. The more you do, the less expensive it is likely to be. However, locating birth parents and making an adoption plan can be emotionally exhausting. If you're not sure how much of the work you can handle yourself, you might try to find a service that offers a range of possibilities to adopters from simple advice to full service and, while signing on for a few services, verify that you can obtain more if you need them later.

c. USING A DOMESTIC ADOPTION FACILITATION SERVICE

1. "Full service" facilitation

Designated adoption through agencies and some attorney-facilitated adoptions offer many services. Some full-service facilitation businesses also exist. These use their contacts and expertise to help you locate birth parents. They will help you develop the most effective strategy for finding a baby such as preparing a description of your family and placing advertisements where birth parents will read them. Facilitators often search nationwide for birth parents and, when necessary, take care of Interstate Compact requirements.

Finding birth parents has become a sophisticated form of marketing. If you are non-traditional adopters, how you present yourselves may be especially important and facilitator expertise could be very helpful. Because independent newborn adoption is so popular, there is competition for birth parents and having an experienced facilitator's help could be a deciding factor in finding them. Facilitators can also help you screen birth parents and find a good match.

Full service facilitators will guide you through the process of making the adoption plan once you have located birth parents. They can help birth parents obtain counseling if desired and see that all necessary consents to the adoption are obtained by them or through referral to an attorney. They will mediate money and health care issues and advise you on what payments can legally be made on behalf of birth parents. They will help you obtain a home study. A good facilitator is prepared for the possibility that birth parents may decide against the adoption before the child is placed with the adoptive family. The facilitator can guide adopters through this turn of events, refer them for counseling, and support and help them locate a new birth family. If all goes well, facilitators will assist in the transition of the baby from birth parents to the adoptive home. They will help adopters arrange for a post-placement study and oversee the legal work of completing the adoption. They may also mediate future contact, if any, between birth family and adoptive family.

Full service facilitation has a lot in common with agency adoption, with a few important exceptions. Here an agency plays no role in screening the adoptive family. Any screening is done by the birth parents and through the home study which can be undertaken by anyone legally authorized to do

148

it in the state where the adopters reside. The terms of the adoption plan are set by birth and adoptive families, not by agency policy. And the child goes directly from birth parent custody to that of the adoptive family without an agency assuming legal guardianship.

2. Partial facilitation

You can arrange an independent adoption by acting as your own facilitator, hiring people to carry out the tasks described in the section on full service facilitation. This role isn't for everyone. It may save money, but it will cost you time and effort. For adopters who have already adopted independently and wish to try again, for those who feel comfortable screening birth families and professionals, and for those who are alert to the issues and risks in adoption, partial facilitation can be an appropriate choice. In some adoptions, such as relative and stepparent adoption, partial facilitation makes a lot of sense. If you are a first-time adopter seeking a healthy newborn however, it is best to stick to agency or full service facilitation.

If you opt for partial facilitation, be aware of some important issues. Many states have restrictions on how adoption is practiced. Advertising for birth parents is illegal in some states, subject to strict limitations in others. Before any payment is made to a birth mother, you need to be certain it is lawful and/or any required authorization has been obtained. If you are seeking a completely open adoption, you can work directly with birth parents to create an adoption plan, but if you wish to retain some confidentiality and not share identifying information, you will need someone to act as an intermediary, to screen phone calls, letters, and to arrange meetings. Because you need to be absolutely certain that birth parents are under no pressure to make an adoption plan, and because their decision has such strong consequences for all of you, it is always best to use a professional intermediary to negotiate with birth parents even in the most open adoption.

3. How to evaluate a domestic adoption facilitator

As with an agency, ask facilitators to send you written materials on their services first. Attorneys with large adoption practices often have them. Then follow up with the questions listed in Checklist #3.

d. AVOIDING ADOPTION FRAUD

You should be aware of adoption fraud, a relatively new scam that arises only in independent open adoption. If you opt for a high degree of openness, you need to take precautions. There are steps you can take to protect yourself:

(a) If you are using a facilitator, check their references carefully.

(b) Verify the pregnancy. Ask for a letter from the birth mother's doctor confirming the pregnancy, due date, and health of the mother and child to the extent known. Once you obtain the letter, call to verify that the doctor is indeed a practitioner, and wrote it. Or you or your intermediary might accompany the birth mother to the doctor for an examination and obtain assurance from the doctor that the mother is indeed pregnant, the due date, and any other relevant facts.

(c) Ask the birth mother for personal and/or employment references and verify them.

(d) Let the birth parents know that you are aware of state adoption laws and that you intend to comply with them.

(e) If you are allowed to pay certain expenses such as medical bills, make arrangements for you to be given copies of the bills so you can verify each before paying for it.

Certain indications may signal potential fraud. A birth mother who appears to lack any connection to her own family may not be what she appears to be. Some work in tandem with a boyfriend. Their aim is usually money; most will seek

CHECKLIST #3
QUESTIONS TO ASK A DOMESTIC ADOPTION FACILITATOR

1. Describe any eligibility criteria you have for adopters. (There may be limitations for some services; others may ask for a valid home study or proof of income.)

2. Describe your services to adopters.

3. What services do you provide to birth parents?

4. How many successful adoptions have you facilitated in each of the past three years?

5. How many for adopters who resemble our family?

6. How long has your service been in existence?

7. What training, skills, and experience does your staff have in adoption?

8. On average, how often do birth parents decide against adoption? What happens to our fees if that occurs?

9. Describe your fee structure. (Must a retainer be paid? Will you be billed by the hour or be asked to pay a lump sum?)

10. What happens to fees we have paid if we decide not pursue a particular adoption?

11. Which, if any, fees are refundable?

12. What additional services will we have to obtain and pay for elsewhere?

13. Can you help us obtain adoption insurance?

14. What is the highest overall fee adopters have paid when using your service? The lowest?

15. When must fees be paid? Can they be amortized?

16. Can we negotiate a lower fee by taking on some tasks ourselves?

17. How do you obtain and evaluate professional assistance such as legal and medical services, counseling, and home study preparation to which you refer adopters?

18. Can you mediate between birth parents and us if and when we don't agree on an issue?

19. What is the average time adopters like our family are likely to wait before a successful placement is made? (Answer should be general.)

20. What happens if the child dies or is born with a disability?

21. Do you facilitate support groups for waiting adopters? If not, can you refer me to one?

22. Has your service been or is it currently involved in a lawsuit over an adoption? If yes, please explain.

23. Can you give me the names of three families I can talk to who have adopted through your service in the past year?

24. Can you refer me to a birth mother who has placed her child through your service? (One of the best recommendations a facilitator can get is from a birth mother who is satisfied that she was served well. Talking to a birth mother can also give you a unique perspective on adoption. It may be hard to ask questions of someone you hope will be placing her child with you. But a birth mother with no connection to you personally may be able to respond to your concerns better than anyone else.)

unauthorized payments early on in your association. Some move from state to state and don't appear to reside anywhere for more than a few months. Avoid any situation in which important facts are withheld from you for whatever reason.

Be honest about your concerns, but be sensitive. Most birth mothers are caring individuals, making the best choices they can under very difficult life circumstances. The number of con artists is very few relative to the number of honest birth parents. Be careful, not suspicious, and you should avoid problems.

e. WHERE INDEPENDENT ADOPTION IS ILLEGAL

At present, six states outlaw independent (non-agency) adoptions in most or all cases: Colorado, Connecticut, Delaware, Massachusetts, Michigan, and Minnesota. In Colorado, Massachusetts, and Michigan, adoptions in which birth parents designate an adoptive family to receive their child are allowed. However, an agency acts as an intermediary in these cases. Some states will permit an independent adoption if it is found to be in the child's best interest, a process in which a judge must be persuaded to waive the agency requirement. Some adopters in these states have changed their residency temporarily in order to adopt a child in a state where independent adoption is allowed. Provided residency and any other legal requirements are observed, this step may be permitted. However, such maneuvers are not looked on favorably by many judges and adoption professionals.

In some cases, adopters have arranged to bring a birth mother to their state to give birth when the mother's state bans independent adoption, or simply to avoid the workings of the Interstate Compact, described in chapter 2. However, many in the adoption community feel that persuading a birth mother to change her residency is problematic, even unethical, especially if she is giving birth in a state where she has no

153

family or support system. The process is likely to be difficult enough for her without adding this additional stress.

Before deciding to pursue one of these alternatives, make sure that an agency adoption really can't meet your family's needs. It will be simpler to choose a traditional agency adoption if one is available, not to mention much cheaper. Whenever the Interstate Compact must be invoked or someone's residency is changed, costs and adoption fees rise significantly. Check out your state's agencies carefully. Some may have reciprocal programs with agencies in other states which can help you locate a child and widen your options.

If you decide an agency adoption isn't right for you, locate adopters who have carried out designated adoptions, or obtained a waiver (ask an adoptive parent group for references). Weigh the pros and cons. Ask agencies which have mediated designated adoptions to describe their role. What support do they provide in any post-placement difficulties that arise? For any of the above alternatives, I strongly recommend that you retain an experienced adoption attorney to guide you through the process.

f. POST-PLACEMENT AND FINALIZATION

If you adopt domestically, post-placement should be straightforward and you should be able to have your study done by whomever did your home study, if you wish. Post-placement studies vary in cost, so compare fees first. Your public adoption agency is a good place to start. If your state allows a home study after a child is placed in your home, the two processes can be combined.

Because you are adopting independently, finalization is up to you. In a domestic adoption, finalization is needed to make you the legal parents of the child. Your attorney/facilitator should handle the legal process.

154

g. USING AN INTERNATIONAL ADOPTION FACILITATOR

Services provided by international adoption facilitators resemble those of most adoption agencies that place foreign-born children. However, few are subject to government regulation. Most specialize in one country or area of the world and confine their service to putting you in contact with a source for a referral, helping you prepare your adoption dossier and prepare for travel if it is required. Facilitators may work with attorneys abroad as well as foster care providers, social workers, and orphanages.

Even when using an independent facilitator, adopters must obtain a home study prepared by a licensed adoption agency in order to meet INS requirements. Many agencies are willing to prepare home studies for independent international adoptions. Choose, if possible, an agency with a program in the country you are adopting from, since they will know the kind of information needed for a home study there. In addition, you will need to arrange by yourself for a post-placement study and readoption once you come home with your child. Your facilitator may be able to help.

International facilitators range from dedicated professionals with much knowledge and experience of the country they work with to mere agents for individual attorneys in other countries. Some facilitators are attorneys themselves or social workers. In countries that lack a system to oversee adoption practice, some facilitators are probably engaging in black market adoption. Because a single U.S. adoption can provide a facilitator in a developing country with a small fortune, the temptation to bend or break the law can be strong. It is up to you as adopters to verify that any facilitator you use is acting legally and ethically. While it may seem like a lot of trouble, ask yourself how you will feel when you have to tell your child how he or she came to be placed for adoption. Children should be able to know for certain that they were adopted because their parents could not care for them. They should not have to live with the possibility that they were stolen or sold in order to be placed with any family, however loving. If you can't find the means to do so, you should not proceed with the adoption, or adopt instead through an international adoption agency program.

Checklist #4 provides questions you can ask a potential international facilitator, and the following information will help guide you through the process.

1. Steps to an ethical, independent adoption

It can help to tell the facilitator and attorney in the child's country that you are interested only in a completely legal, ethical adoption. You can make it clear that you will not follow through on an illegal adoption and that you are prepared to wait a little longer to ensure that the child is legally free and that any other legal requirements have been met.

(a) Learn about the country

If possible, choose a country you are familiar with. If you speak the language, even a little, that can help. Do a library periodical search for news magazine articles on adoption and read about the country you are considering. Is it in the midst of social and political upheaval? Has there been an adoption scandal there recently? Rent and watch a travel video or check one out from the library. Since you will, in effect, be adopting the country as well as the child, now is the time to explore how you feel about it. Find someone who comes from the country and discuss adoption with them. See the Resource Guide for this chapter and for chapter 12 for more tips on learning about your child's country.

(b) Don't make unwarranted assumptions

Below are five false assumptions often made by international adopters. Believing these fallacies has led adopters into illegal and unethical adoptions and sometimes to adoption cancellation.

CHECKLIST #4
QUESTIONS TO ASK AN INTERNATIONAL ADOPTION FACILITATOR

First, ask for and review carefully any written material they have on their services. Talk to adopters who used this service before. I recommend that you not use any facilitator for whom you cannot obtain any non-adopter references or who has no track record. If you are not familiar with the country you are adopting from, and if this is your first adoption, it is especially important to verify the bona fides of your facilitator before proceeding further.

No questions are included about special needs adoption. If you seek to adopt a special needs child from another country, I recommend that you do so only through an agency with a program that includes medical evaluation of the children before referrals are made and that offers or refers post-placement and post-finalization services and support to the adoptive family.

1. Describe adopter eligibility criteria, if any, for the country.

2. Describe the services you provide to adopters. What is your objective in offering these services?

3. Describe your connection to the country from which you place children. How did you come to facilitate adoptions from this country? What is your history and experience with the country? (Some facilitators are dual citizens with strong connections to the country of their birth and a knowledge of the language. Others may be successful adoptive parents who formed ties with the country of their child's birth. Still others may be former adoption agency employees who have struck out on their own. Any of these may be operating legally and ethically or not. But knowing their background can help you know where to seek further information about the facilitator's operations.)

4. How do you come to be aware of the children who need parents?

5. Are you familiar with the adoption laws of the country? What are they?

6. Are the country's adoption laws changing or about to be changed? Is the country a signatory to the Hague Convention? (Signatory countries can be expected to change their adoption laws in the near future. Sending countries are likely to limit or prohibit independent international adoptions, so the answer to this question is important.)

7. How many placements have you facilitated from this country overall? How many for each of the last three years?

8. How many placements have you facilitated for each of the last three years with a family that resembles ours?

9. Do you speak the language of the country? Well? If not, how do you communicate with adoption professionals, foster families, or court personnel abroad?

10. Who are your contacts in the country? How have you determined that they are operating ethically? Describe how you work together.

11. (For a facilitator who is a lawyer in the child's country) Do you also conduct adoptions for residents of your country? If not, why not? (Some lawyers do adoptions only for wealthy foreigners, knowing that local families cannot afford the high fees. If a lawyer only acts for foreigners, this is not a sign of illegality per se, but it is cause for further investigation.)

12. Can you give me two professional references? (These would be from colleagues of the facilitator, or a licensing authority such as a bar association or social work professional organization. Other adoptive families are not in a position to know what the facilitator's standing is in his or her profession.)

13. When a referral is offered to us, what information will we be given to help us make a decision? (Photos, video, nothing?)

14. Can we specify the child's gender?

15. What will be the racial/cultural background of the child? (Be wary of a facilitator who guarantees children of a certain race.)

16. Describe your fee structure. When must fees be paid? Can they be amortized? (I strongly advise against paying all of your fees in advance of traveling to the country. In addition to making yourself vulnerable to fraud, there are many factors beyond the facilitator's control that can affect the adoption outcome. If the country restricts adoptions or changes the law, you may be unable to recover fees paid. I have never heard of U.S. adopters recovering fees paid to international facilitators for adoptions which fell through.)

17. Please explain what your fee covers. (Be sure to compare the fee charged with others, such as those set out in the *ICCC Handbook*. Not only is an exceptionally high fee no guarantee of high quality, it may be a sign of illegality.)

18. How can I pay the fee? Can I transfer funds electronically to a bank in the country? Send a cashier's check? A money order?

19. Once I have accepted a referral, what happens to the child until I can bring him or her home? If the child is in an orphanage who pays, if any payment is needed? If the child is living in the birth family or a foster home, how is the child supported? (In some cases you may be asked to pay for prior care given before you accepted the referral. Before doing so, find out who has supported the child up to now and verify that the money asked for will go to repay the upkeep of the child.)

20. What will my foster care payments be applied to? (Infant formula, food, clothes, medical care?)

21. How can I communicate with the birth or foster family? Can you give us their address? If I write a letter can it be delivered to them?

22. If the child is with the birth family, will this be an open adoption?

23. Can I meet with the birth family and arrange for future contact? (The Hague Convention will prohibit pre-adoption contact between birth and adoptive families.) Can I obtain information about the family's medical and social history?

24. How long must I stay in the country?

25. How many trips must I make?

26. At the time I am asked to travel, will the adoption be approved or is there a possibility that it won't be allowed?

27. Has a family in an adoption you facilitated ever traveled to the country and returned without a child? Why?

28. Will I have to travel before receiving a referral?

29. (For couples) Must we both travel? Both remain in the country for the entire process? Can we bring other children in our family?

30. What is the average wait for a referral for adopters like us?

31. What is the average wait between accepting a referral and placement?

32. What happens if we travel to the country and the child is not who we expected? What happens to the child?

33. How do you locate families for children? (Do they advertise in reputable adoption publications? In city newspapers?)

34. What services can you help us obtain for the adoption in this country? (Referral to a reputable translator; help in dealing with the country's embassy or consulate; help in putting together your dossier; help in arranging travel.)

35. What services can you help us obtain in the country we are traveling to? (Interpreter, accommodation, lawyer, tourist information.)

36. How do you select a lawyer/foster family/interpreter/orphanage to work with? (Are they the facilitator's relatives or professional colleagues?)

37. How do we communicate with you and/or anyone we need to contact in the country? Can you interpret for us over the telephone or do you know someone who can?

38. Have you ever been involved in a lawsuit in this country or the country from which you are placing children? Please describe.

39. Can you give me references for three families who have adopted with your help during the past year?

- **Fallacy #1:** All fees charged are reasonable
  and warranted.

Too often, fees in international adoption are set solely on the basis of what the intermediary feels adopters can be persuaded to pay. Never pay a fee to an agency or intermediary without first comparing it to other fees charged for the same service. The *ICCC Handbook* lists agency programs and fees by country. If your source is charging much more than other sources, ask some questions before choosing it. Seek a breakdown of expenses from intermediaries. Lawyers in every country are expected to give an accounting to their clients.

Sometimes facilitators seek additional payments beyond what has been agreed on. Faced with such demands, adopters usually pay whatever is asked if they can afford to, feeling that to say no would mean jeopardizing the placement. Rarely is confirmation of the need for payment sought. How can you avoid this in your adoption? Agree with your facilitator from the beginning what fees are to be paid for the entire adoption. Ask for receipts for any additional expenses you are expected to pay or reinburse prior to payment.

- **Fallacy #2:** You have to bribe officials to get anything
  done.

Bribery exists in every country including our own — and it is also highly illegal. In every country there are also many ethical lawyers, judges, civil servants, and parents who would not dream of taking or paying a bribe. Many countries are working hard to stamp out corruption. You do not have to pay a single bribe, in money or in "gifts," to anyone to conduct a legal adoption, nor should you.

- **Fallacy #3:** There are so many homeless children
  that no one must care what happens to them.

Most of the supposedly homeless children in developing countries do have family ties, albeit loose ones. Many countries are engaged in ambitious programs to advance the health, education, and future prospects of their children. In some of these countries, despite widespread poverty, domestic adoption is far more common than in our own and the society as a whole loves and values children.

- **Fallacy #4:** Any child is better off being adopted by North Americans than remaining in such poverty.

A child may or may not be better off in an adoptive North American home. But in any event, we are not in a position to judge this at the time we make adoption decisions. This rescue myth obscures the important truth of adoption that we saw in chapter 1. Adoption is built on losses. Losing biological parents and a whole culture is a genuine loss, never to be lightly dismissed. In the United States, one of the world's richest countries, 21% of all children live below the poverty line. If we were judged by the same standards we use to judge much poorer countries, we would have a hard time demonstrating that children are better off here than elsewhere.

- **Fallacy #5:** Cash-only adoptions are acceptable.

Any international adoption in which you are asked to make payments in cash only is questionable. Seattle adoption educator and mother of two Brazilian children, Joan Ramos, observes that in our global economy, every country has the means to execute electronic transfers of funds from one bank to another. However, these transactions may alert government authorities to the transfer. In an illegal adoption, or one in which an unconscionably large fee is paid by the adopters, facilitators anxious to prevent the authorities from learning of the transaction will seek to avoid leaving a paper trail. They may simply wish to avoid paying income tax or complying with other laws, or they may actually be engaging in illegal adoptions. In any case, you should never have to provide large payments in cash. *If your facilitator and/or attorney will not accept a cashier's check, electronic transfer, or any other payment except cash, you should cancel the adoption.* Reputable facilitators, attorneys, and adoption agencies do not make such demands. Some adopters are told that the country's economy is so unstable that only cash is acceptable. This is not a valid argument. Even in countries with out-of-control inflation, the American dollar is a stable currency and a payment made electronically or by cashier's check is acceptable.

(c) The importance of references

The best tool for verifying the bona fides of an international facilitator is good references from a knowledgeable source. Talking with adoptive parents who have used the facilitator, while helpful and recommended, is not enough. Other adopters may not have been in a position to assess the legality of their adoption any more than you are. Adopters in a foreign country, especially those with little experience of foreign travel and who don't speak the language, have to depend on the facilitator for their knowledge of what's going on. The facilitator is unlikely to confide to the adopter that she is bribing the judge or that someone has been hired to pose as the birth mother of the child to be adopted. Yet these things have happened.

Before committing to an international facilitator, contact a national adoption organization such as AFA, ICCC, NAIC, or, if you are exploring Latin America, LAAF and LAPA. LAAF publishes fact sheets on each country that permits international adoption. Some of the larger adoption agencies may be able to provide you with information. If the facilitator is located in the source country, you can ask them to tell you the name and address of any professional organizations they belong to. (Attorneys will certainly belong to one; so may social workers.) Telephone or write to the organization and ask if the facilitator is indeed a member in good standing.

Another possibility is to call the country's embassy and ask if they have received any complaints about the facilitator. The U.S. State Department may also be able to offer suggestions about verifying a facilitator's bona fides. In Canada, the National Adoption Desk may be able to help you with queries about countries where they have an existing program. Even if the facilitator is unlicensed, if they are operating locally, your state adoption authority may have information about them along with the attorney general and Better Business Bureau. If the facilitator works with families in a different state, find out which one(s) and contact the state licenser and adoptive parent groups there, too.

(d) Working with the Immigration and Naturalization Service

Once you have chosen a facilitator, you will need to assemble your INS dossier, requirements for which are described in chapter 2. You will need to know the country you are adopting from and the facilitator you are using in order to fill out the I-600A form for advance processing. It is not necessary to have a particular child in mind at this stage.

Some time after you have turned in the I-600A form, fees, and supporting documents, the INS will send you a notice saying that your dossier is now in the hands of the U.S. embassy or consulate in charge of issuing visas for children adopted in the country you have chosen. If you have not received this notice within 12 weeks, contact the INS and verify that they are working on your dossier. Cases have been reported in which adoption dossiers have been misplaced for months until adopters have queried their whereabouts. Once you have received the notice, apart from obtaining your passport if you don't already have one, you should not have to deal with INS again until after the adoption. If a year passes without a placement occurring, you will need to retrace your steps.

(e) Foster care abroad

While many children live in an orphanage until placement, others reside with birth or foster families. You may be asked to contribute to the cost of foster care, usually in monthly increments. It may take up to a year or even longer after a child is identified for you before placement, so it is important to establish that your child's environment is safe and at a minimum provides sufficient nurture. Some countries require that adopters make two trips to complete an adoption. There, adopters have an opportunity to check out the child's living situation and verify that foster care payments are being used for the benefit of the child.

Many foster families become very attached to the children they care for. These families are a part of your child's heritage. Especially where ties to the birth family are weak or non-existent, the foster family may form an important link to your child's culture and past. Good foster care is a better alternative than even the best orphanage since the child is part of a family and receives individual attention that orphanage staff seldom have time to provide. However, in poor countries it sometimes happens that foster care payments are siphoned off by facilitators, attorneys, or intermediaries and little reaches the foster child. Foster parents may use payments to support their whole family and apply little if anything to the care of the child.

To avoid poor foster care, make sure your facilitator knows that you feel high-quality care is very important. One possibility is to ask for the address of the foster family and write to them. Send them pictures of your family and tell them that you appreciate the care they are taking of your child. Let them know that you intend to meet with them and discuss your child when you travel to adopt. Reluctance by the facilitator to put you in direct contact with the foster family could mean that foster care is inadequate and/or that your money is not going to the foster family.

Research what it costs to raise a child in this country. A world fact book in the reference section of your library will have the information. If the minimum wage is $50 per month and the average global family income is $100 per month, you should not be paying $400 per month in foster care for one child. On the other hand, if you wish your child to be fed with high-quality infant formula, a payment of $150 a month may well be warranted.

If you are asked to pay a suspiciously high amount in foster care, it is almost certainly a sign that the money is being used for something other than or in addition to foster care. Try to strike a balance between high and low payment. Ultimately, your child should live with a family whose aim is to provide good care, not to earn a living from the foster care.

(f) Readoption in the United States

Aside from the exceptions noted in chapter 2, international adoptions are carried out in the child's birth country. Once the child is brought to the United States, the adoptive family should readopt (see chapter 2). Foreign-born adoptees are admitted to the United States on the basis of the visa issued for them by the U.S. government. Shortly after entry, they receive a "green card," a resident alien permit authorizing them to reside in the country for a stated period of time.

The child's ability to become a citizen depends on a court first determining that the adoption decree is valid. If the only decree is from another country, the chance exists that it will not be considered sufficient to permit the child to obtain citizenship. Readoption means that the child now has proof of adoption valid throughout the United States and can count on being naturalized. Unfortunately, many adopters fail to readopt their children in the U.S., so their children live in a citizenship limbo. If the adopters are unable to care for the child or the adoption disrupts, the chance exists that the child could be deported.

If your adoption is wholly independent, you will need to arrange readoption on your own. Assuming your adoption was straightforward, you may be able to accomplish this without the help of a lawyer if your state allows self-representation. The state court with jurisdiction over adoption should be able to tell you what is needed for readoption. You will also need to have your

166

adoption decree, the child's birth certificates, and any other foreign court documents translated into English. (First ask the court if they have requirements for translator credentials.) You will need a valid post-placement study as well, done by someone authorized to do such a study in your state for an independent international adoption. While a home study for an international adoption must be carried out by a licensed agency, this is not a requirement for post-placement studies, unless it is required by your state's law.

If you decide to retain a lawyer to help you readopt, compare fees carefully. Some attorneys charge large fees for what is usually a simple, straightforward matter. You may be able to arrange for a lawyer to review your documents and plan for a reduced fee, after you prepare the paperwork. Many adoptive parents have readopted without a lawyer's help and can guide you through the process. You might also place an advertisement in an adoptive parent newsletter or national adoption publication asking for advice from successful readopters.

Some international adopters have run into problems when their adoptions didn't take place through the usual channels. Parents adopting special needs children who were admitted into the U.S. on medical visas to expedite needed surgical procedures have occasionally discovered that re-adoption for them is much more complicated. In such a case, seek the advice of an experienced *immigration* attorney. Most adoption attorneys handle only domestic adoptions and are unused to handling immigration questions, lack familiarity with immigration law, and don't know the individuals who make and execute immigration policy decisions. If your re-adoption runs into a snag because of an immigration question, ask your state bar association for referrals to immigration attorneys or get a referral from an adoptive parent group. If your community has a legal clinic which offers immigration advice, they may also be able to refer you to someone with expertise in the field.

(g) Post-placement

For international adoptions, you may be able to have the agency that did your home study do the post-placement study, too. However, in some areas, post-placement studies for independent international adoptions must be carried out in accordance with separate rules. Call your local court before arranging for a post-placement study and verify procedures.

h. RECORDKEEPING FOR AN INDEPENDENT ADOPTION

Recordkeeping for an independent domestic adoption is much the same as recordkeeping for an agency adoption, with a few exceptions (see the section on recordkeeping in chapter 7.) If your facilitator is an attorney, as most are, you will most likely be billed as work is done. Keep track of what you are billed for and verify that it was in fact done. If you are not certain about what a bill means, ask for clarification. If you are paying for birth parent expenses, make sure that you have a record of what you have paid and what it was used for. You should be able to prove later that any money paid on account of birth parents was legal and warranted. If you are asked to pay for something about which you are uncertain, ask your facilitator to confirm that it is valid and warranted before paying it. Then get a receipt for everything you pay on account of birth parents which indicates what the receipt is for.

If you are adopting internationally, you are likely to accumulate an enormous pile of documents. To keep on top of all the paper and be able to access it easily, it is worth taking the time to develop a handy recordkeeping system. Check the section on agency recordkeeping in chapter 7 for further ideas.

In any adoption, but especially an independent international one, think big when ordering copies of important documents such as birth certificates. You will almost certainly need more copies than you imagine. If you were born out of state, you will probably have to order certified copies of birth certificates by mail. I recommend ordering at least three copies of any document; a case can even be made for five copies. Copies of many documents will be needed for the INS as well as for your international dossier. If you are working with more than one source at once, or if you are seeking to adopt two or more children, you will need twice as many of every document. Order at least three signed and notarized copies of your home study. Many people (myself included) have had to frantically locate duplicate documents at the last minute; but I've never heard adopters complain that they had too many copies of anything.

When assembling an adoption dossier, be sure that you retain original documents of everything in the dossier. That way, if the dossier is misplaced, you can send a new one without being set back several months.

Don't throw anything away! You may need it later. A reference to an attorney you decided against using could prove important if another source dries up. I kept the slip of paper on which I wrote down the brief sketchy information about our daughter I first received over the telephone from our Brazilian attorney. It now forms part of her life book.

RESOURCE GUIDE

1. Books about independent open adoption

Lindsay, Jeanne Warren. *Open Adoption: A Caring Option.*
Buena Park, CA: Morning Glory, 1987.

Rappaport, Bruce M. *The Open Adoption Book: A Guide to Adoption Without Tears.* New York: Macmillan, 1992.

Rillera, Mary Jo and Sharon Kaplan. *Cooperative Adoption.* 2nd ed.
Westminster, CA: Triadoption Publications, 1985

2. Books about independent adoption

Michelman, Stanley B. and Meg Schneider. *Private Adoption Handbook: A Step-by-Step Guide to the Legal, Emotional and Practical Demands of adopting a Baby.* New York: Dell, 1988.

Sullivan, Michael R. and Susan Schultz. *Adopt the Baby You Want.* New York: Simon & Schuster, 1990.

3. Resources for international adoption

Heilbroner, Robert L. *The Great Ascent.* New York: Harper and Row, 1963.

ICCC Handbook. (See chapter 3 Resource Guide.)

Register, Cheri. *Are Those Kids Yours?* New York: The Free Press, 1991

TIPS

Before you commit to an independent newborn adoption, learn about the opposing views on this very controversial issue. No other form of adoption has so polarized the adoption community. Expose yourself to the opinions of groups such as Concerned United Birth Parents, as well as to the enthusiastic supporters of independent placement. As with many divisive issues, all sides have valid concerns and opinions. Most tragedies that have occurred to adoptive families who saw beloved children removed from their homes were preventable. In virtually every case, the adoptive family was poorly informed about the legal and ethical issues of independent adoption and made unnecessary errors.

Some excellent guidebooks for developing countries exist. Lonely Planet, Moon Publications Inc., and APA Insight Guides are good sources. The Central American and South American Handbooks are thorough resources for Latin America. Look for guides that discuss a country's history, political system, geography, customs, and culture. Guidebooks geared to tourists spending a week or two in capital cities or tourist spots will have little to offer.

9

STEPPARENT ADOPTION

a. WHY INCLUDE STEPPARENTS IN A BOOK ON ADOPTION?

About half of all first marriages end in divorce, as do two-thirds of second marriages with children. The increasing numbers of unwed mothers who later form new families in or outside of marriage add to the total. Today, about 50 million Americans live in some form of stepfamily — nearly one-fifth of the total population.

Thousands of stepparent adoptions take place each year in the United States, but few written resources exist for stepparents considering adoption. Most writers on adoption address only non-relative adopters, while books for stepparents concentrate on the social issues arising from the blending of two families. Yet stepparent adoptions are thought to comprise more than half of the adoptions that take place each year in the United States and stepfamilies represent a fast growing segment of the population.

One difference between stepparent and non-relative adoption is that in the former there is usually a living biological parent who has had and continues to have a relationship, however limited, with the child. Because the stepparent is married to one of the child's biological parents, other options besides adoption, such as legal guardianship or custody, are available. This chapter addresses custodial stepparents, since non-custodial stepparents rarely adopt.

All adoptions raise universal issues. A biological father or mother are ceasing to be legal parents and a differently configured set are becoming the socially acknowledged parents. The issues of loss and gain that we examined in chapter 1 exist for all children whether or not they are adopted by relatives and stepparents. The high failure rate of second marriages with children testifies to the inherent stresses in blended families. "Father" and "Mother" are terms loaded with social and emotional meanings. For stepparents and relatives who parent children they did not give birth to, options besides adoption do exist. But when adoption is considered and selected, it is important to understand the ramifications of the decision. It is unquestionably right for some families in some circumstances; but even where it is, it is important for adopters to understand that they are joining a wide class of adopters in our society beyond other stepparents and family members. Issues such as legislation that affects adoption, deduction of adoption expenses for tax purposes, and legal assistance in adopting will affect many of these parents. The purpose of including stepparents and relatives in this book is to help you see the issues adoption raises, decide if it's the right decision for your family and, if so, how best to accomplish it.

Additionally, non-relative adoption is growing to resemble relative and stepparent adoption. A majority of newborn and older children adoptions, including those born internationally, are semi- or completely open. More adopters also find themselves grappling with issues such as maintaining and mediating contact between birth and adoptive families. Today more than ever, all adopters have something to teach and learn from each other.

b. SPECIAL CONSIDERATIONS

1. Stepmothers

Stepmothers have a very long history. In the days when women often died in childbirth leaving motherless infants and toddlers, men commonly remarried as soon as possible to provide for the children's care. These wives usually went on to have more children. The emotional and psychological disruptions for the family were undoubtedly significant and even traumatic, which helps to explain why many cultures produced fairy tales in which a "good" biological mother is replaced by a "wicked" stepmother. These stories spoke to the experience of children losing a parent suddenly and having to adjust to a new one before resolving their grief.

For much of the 20th century, most children remained with their biological mother and most stepparents were stepfathers. Since the 1970s, however, fathers have sought custody more frequently in divorce cases. Despite a popular perception that children nearly always go to the mother when custody is disputed, in fact, where they actively seek it, fathers are awarded custody about 63% of the time. By 1988, 11% of stepfamilies were headed by biological fathers and stepmothers and the number of custodial stepmothers continues to increase. Yet nearly all stepparent adoptions are carried out by stepfathers.

Custodial stepmothers, it seems, rarely adopt their stepchildren. This even holds true where the father is widowed and no biological mother exists. Some professionals are concerned that the lack of a sense of entitlement to parent can prevent a stepmother from taking the step of adopting a stepchild even when she is the primary or only mother figure in the child's life.

2. Evaluating the options

In some cases, adoption may not be the best option for a family. But whatever their choice, custodial stepparents need to consider whether their relationship with the stepchild is adequately protected. If there is a strong or even only intermittent relationship with the biological mother (or father), adoption may not be advisable. After all, adoption severs the legal ties of responsibility with the birth parent. In cases where the biological parent has disappeared, withdrawn from any contact, died, or where the child was an infant when the separation occurred, forming a legal adoptive bond may be the best option for building the child's permanent family. Even where full adoption is rejected, seeking an order of legal guardianship or joint custody with the biological parent will give additional protection to the relationship.

(a) Legal consequences

One way to approach this issue is to ask "what will happen to my stepchild if my partner (the biological parent) dies or is disabled?" This is a question you should be able to answer one way or another. If you have not legally adopted your stepchild, the child may not automatically inherit from your estate. A child who is estranged from a biological parent may not inherit under that parent's will, either. Adoption automatically puts you on the same footing as a biological parent. However, even if you choose an option that falls short of full adoption, there are steps you can take to protect your stepchild. Consulting an estate planner will help you to evaluate your legal choices.

Every family is different and there are no absolute legal or other guidelines as to who should adopt. Several factors can help clarify the picture. First, if a living biological parent is alive, in nearly all cases they will have to consent for the adoption to take place. The trend is for courts to prevent adoption where a biological parent objects. While there are cases where courts override a non-custodial biological parent's objections and grant an adoption, these often involve lengthy litigation, emotional trauma, and significant expense. Litigation can continue for years while the status of the family remains in legal limbo. Where the non-custodial parent objects, here again legal guardianship or custody may prove a better alternative.

Children above a certain age must consent to the adoption. They may have divided feelings whether or not they have a relationship with the non-custodial parent. Children whose consent is needed to a stepparent adoption will usually be asked to speak with a judge privately to give their views on whether they wish to be adopted.

Some stepparents have been required to contribute toward family and child support when the stepfamily separates, even though they have no custodial rights to the child. Whatever your adoption decision, as a stepparent, you and your family will be better off if you take steps to protect your relationship and learn what your rights and responsibilities are with respect to each alternative.

(b) Emotional and psychological consequences

Stepparents exist in a cultural limbo. Not felt to be "real" parents to their stepchildren, often not acquiring legal parental or guardian status (especially in the case of stepmothers), and rarely if at all included among the population of adopters, it can be very hard for stepparents to find their place as parents.

Although gender-based roles are in transition, we still tend to ascribe different jobs and characteristics to a mother and father. Thus, a custodial stepmother is likely to form a strong bond with her stepchild, especially if she plays a traditional homemaker role. Her relationship to her stepchild may require some legal definition to protect it from future disruptions. Let's suppose a stepmother marries a man who has custody of his 18-month old son. The stepmother stays home and parents this child and later has a biological daughter. If this marriage ends in divorce, as two out of three will, the stepmother may find she has no parental rights with respect to her stepson. Many courts would not entertain a request from her for sole or shared custody, or even visitation rights. She could parent the boy for years and the children could form strong sibling bonds — and yet the end result could still be that when the second marriage ends, she loses any right to stay in her stepson's life.

For stepmothers considering whether or not to seek adoption, it may help to frame the question as if you were the stepfather. If you were the child's stepfather, would you want to adopt? If the answer is yes, take another look at adoption yourself.

c.   LEGAL REQUIREMENTS

Each state has its own requirements. Stepparents must meet the definition of who may adopt. The consent of the non-custodial biological parent is needed. In limited circumstances, consent may be dispensed with. If so, the issue must be resolved prior to consideration of the adoption. If the child is 10 or over, (depending on the child's state of residence) the child must consent as well. Some states require the consent of the non-adopting custodial biological parent; others simply require that parent to join in the adoption petition.

The procedural requirements are usually relaxed in stepparent adoption. In most states, a home study is not required. The waiting period before the adoption can be finalized may be curtailed or omitted and, in some states, the hearing dispensed with. The Interstate Compact does not apply to stepparent adoptions where the child is moving from the custody of a biological parent in one state to the other parent and stepparent in another state. If the child has been residing with a grandparent, adult sibling, aunt, uncle, or legal guardian, a stepparent adoption should be exempt from the ICPC as well.

If it appears that adoption will be problematic because a necessary consent isn't given, stepparents should carefully review other legal alternatives. Discuss seeking a legal custody or guardianship order with your partner, the other biological parent.

The procedure for seeking such an order differs from state to state. As legal custodian or guardian of a stepchild, while you won't have the exclusivity of the adoptive parent relationship, you will have the right to make parenting decisions for the child. Whatever happens to the marriage, your relationship with your stepchild will have a legal basis.

d. EXTENDED BIRTH FAMILY ISSUES

One issue to consider when looking into stepparent adoption is the role of the non-custodial parent's family. Because adoption severs the legal ties between that parent and the child, grandparents and other relatives will be affected by the process, even though they may have no right to prevent it from taking place. Further, where the biological parent consents to the adoption and has no interest in maintaining a relationship with the child, the grandparents may feel differently. Sometimes a biological parent withholds consent to an adoption out of a desire to preserve the child's relationship with the grandparents.

Increasingly, stepparent and relative adoptions are taking these relationships into account. Just as open adoption agreements may sometimes provide for ongoing contact between birth and adoptive families to survive finalization, it may be possible to provide for ongoing grandparent or other relative contact to survive a stepparent adoption. Offering to provide this may remove a biological parent's objection to a stepparent adoption. Even where consent is not an issue, recognizing that these ties are of value to the child and building them into the adoption can help make the process a harmonious one.

e. WORKING WITH A LAWYER

The simplest way to accomplish a stepparent adoption is to retain an experienced adoption attorney. In a case in which all parties requiring notice and consent are easy to contact and agree to the adoption, the process should be quick and inexpensive. But where a party, especially a biological parent, cannot be located or withholds consent, the process will be more complicated and costly. Because stepparent adoptions are common, lawyers who specialize in family law will be familiar with the process. You can ask your state bar association for references. Before retaining a lawyer, ask about his or her experience with stepparent adoption and whether he or she can advise you on other options such as obtaining guardianship of the child. Review the checklist of questions in chapter 8 and see the Resource Guide at the end of this chapter for other tips.

f. WORKING WITHOUT A LAWYER

1. Making use of free legal resources

In a simple stepparent adoption, retaining a lawyer to represent you may not be necessary. Each jurisdiction has its own rules about pro se (self) representation. Your first step should be to call your court with jurisdiction over adoption and ask if you can do your own stepparent adoption. (If you are not sure which court to go to, call your public adoption agency.) If the answer is yes, ask if they can help you. They may have information packets which outline procedures and provide any forms needed. Ask the clerk if there is someone you can talk to who can give you information on doing your own stepparent adoption. You may also be able to use a local courthouse library and ask the librarian for assistance. (Go to a court which hears family law cases.)

State and local bar associations sometimes dispense free information on simple legal issues. Some operate free telephone information lines. Callers are given basic information and referred to additional resources. If your community has a free legal clinic, contact them and ask if they have any materials on stepparent adoption.

2. Getting summary legal advice

You may be able to obtain summary legal advice to help you do your own adoption. Many bar associations offer a referral service to lawyers with expertise in the area of law you are interested in and who can provide you with a limited amount of advice (half an hour is common) for a low, pre-set fee.

To make the best use of this service, do everything you can on your own first. Contact your court and obtain forms, read about stepparent adoption and verify that you will be able to obtain all needed consents easily. Then, make an appointment with an attorney through a bar referral service. Prepare any questions you can think of ahead of time and put them in writing. Fill out the forms you are planning to file or serve and bring them to show the attorney. Prepare a brief summary (you can write it down and give it to the lawyer to read) describing what you have done so far and what you plan to do to complete the adoption. Ask the lawyer to give you any additional suggestions or advice that can help you accomplish the adoption. You may also want to verify that you can retain this lawyer later, if necessary. In that case, the lawyer will have a head start knowing about your case and subsequent services may be less expensive than for a new lawyer who must be brought up to speed on what's happened so far.

3. Finding free community resources

You can be sure that others have done their own stepparent adoptions. While stepparents are poorly represented in adoptive parent groups, other community groups include many stepparents. Some churches sponsor support groups for blended families. The Stepfamily Foundation provides books as well as audio and video tapes on stepfamily issues, including the law. (See the Resource Guide for details.) Community college and university extension classes often include courses on family-related topics. Obtain a calendar and see if a class for blended families is offered. Extension courses on legal topics are given at times. While not free, these classes are almost always very inexpensive and offer an opportunity to network with others in your situation.

Use community bulletin boards. If you have a computer and modem, try contacting an electronic bulletin board. Call any community center that provides some form of family counseling and see if they can help you locate someone who did their own adoption.

RESOURCE GUIDE

1. Books about stepparenting

Berman, Claire. *Making it as a Stepparent: New Rules, New Roles.* New York: Doubleday, 1980.

Bettelheim, Bruno. *The Uses of Enchantment.* New York: Knopf, 1976.

Einstein, Elizabeth. *The Stepfamily.* Berkeley, CA: Shambala, 1985.

Hodder, Elizabeth. *Stepfamilies.* New York: Gloucester Press, 1990.

Prilik, Pearl Ketover. *Stepmothering.* Los Angeles, CA: Forman Publishing, 1988.

2. Resources for stepparents

- The Stepfamily Foundation
  333 West End Avenue
  New York, NY 10023
  (212) 877-3244

The Stepfamily Foundation provides information and resources on stepparenting to stepfamilies, the professionals who deal with them, and the general public. Membership includes a newsletter and telephone counseling is available. The foundation sells books and audio and video tapes on various issues, including family law.

TIPS

Establish contact and stay in touch with the adoption community. Many of the issues stepparent and non-relative adopters face are similar, especially as children grow older or in the case of open adoption. Issues of loss, a child's sense of divided loyalties, or the desire to search for a biological parent may affect each kind of adoptive family. Groups such as NACAC, AFA, and NAIC can help you keep informed on issues, resources, and conferences on adoption.

To locate other stepfamilies, churches are a good place to begin. Many offer stepparent support groups and may be willing to open participation to non-church members. Family therapists who advertise in the local newspapers may be willing to put you in touch with other stepfamilies. And your state public adoption or child welfare agency can probably help you locate stepfamily support services which exist in your community.

10
RELATIVE ADOPTION

In the years between 1982 and 1992, the United States saw a 40% increase in the number of children who live with their grandparents. Today, grandparents are sole or primary caregivers for over a million children. Two million more live in households that include grandparents and the numbers continue to climb. Children also reside with adult siblings, cousins, aunts and uncles, or in other extended family units. Parents often maintain some involvement that may be erratic and or even disruptive. The causes of parental failure are many: drugs and alcohol, poverty, AIDS, and imprisonment are a few. The growth of relative caregivers is nationwide; no region is unaffected.

a. SPECIAL CONSIDERATIONS

1. Evaluating the options

Like stepparents, relatives have options available besides adopting which may be equally or more beneficial. Adoption needs to be considered only as one choice: not necessarily the best or worst. When it is chosen, however, relative adopters need to be aware of the universality of the issues it raises and how to address them.

2. Legal considerations

Relatives usually become custodial or adoptive parents as a result of a family crisis. One common scenario is that a child is removed from the custody of the biological parents by a child welfare authority which immediately seeks a relative to place the child with. This is usually, though not always, a grandparent. Children who come into care today have greater

181

special needs than in the past, so caring for such children can be expensive, time-consuming, and require considerable parenting expertise.

When you accept custody of a relative's child, you need to obtain quality counseling on your options: legal and financial. You may be eligible for financial assistance for medical expenses and coverage of special needs such as counseling. Increasingly throughout our society, women are in the workforce. As a relative you may also be employed and need to make daycare arrangements. You may be eligible for a daycare subsidy.

At this stage you need to seek a qualified opinion on all your options, including (eventually) legal guardianship or adoption. What are the pros and cons of becoming a licensed foster parent? Many relative caregivers do just that. Whether it is the right choice for your family depends on your state law, your income, lifestyle, the needs of the child, and your personal needs. Perhaps some arrangement short of foster parenting is a better choice. The agency that has placed the child with you should be willing to take the time to inform you of your options and respond fully to questions. You have the right to this information. Overloaded as it is, the child welfare system today would collapse without the assistance of relative caregivers.

Relative support groups report that relatives often feel they owe it to their family members to support them unassisted. Relatives may be unwilling to ask for public assistance with its connotation of poverty and helplessness and decline to seek such support. However, the child may have needs that would be expensive for anyone to fill. It has been noted that the wealthy in our society rarely seem to share such scruples and pay attorneys large fees to identify and obtain any and all benefits and tax breaks to which they might be entitled, however small. Children who come into care more often than not, have some expensive needs to be met. If it is difficult or impossible for you to meet them, you should seek assistance. It is, after all, the child who will suffer most if those needs cannot be met.

3. Emotional and psychological considerations

Most relative primary caregivers and adopters are grandparents. Because of their greater resources and stable lifestyle, when parents can't care for a child they frequently turn to their own parents. Child welfare authorities turn to the child's grandparents, too. Often a pattern develops in which grandparents gradually become caregivers over time. With no advance notice their grandchild is left with them and later picked up just as abruptly by the parent. Sometimes grandparents step in to protect grandchildren they see receiving inadequate care. Or children may be removed from the home by child protection authorities and placed with grandparents. However it comes about, grandparents usually have little control over the process.

Unique to relative adopters — especially grandparents — is the fact that raising and adopting the child is not the result of a planned, self-determined decision. Relatives often feel helpless, forced back into a parenting role they thought they had left behind. They may feel guilty — responsible for the inadequacies of their own children as parents. Sadness for the collapse of the family unit that necessitated their stepping in, must also be faced. Relatives considering adoption need to be fully aware of how these issues are affecting them and how they see the choices they have in providing for the child.

Grandparents and older caregivers often feel left out of the parenting mainstream. It's been a generation, after all, since they raised their own children. Times have changed! Spanking is no longer an acceptable disciplinary technique. Schooling choices are broad and bewildering. Many of these children have special needs. Relatives are often faced with overwhelming problems and must seek information and make decisions that they were utterly unprepared for. Grandparents, looking forward to increased freedom in retirement, instead face years of heavy demands on their time, energy, and financial resources.

In addition, relatives must decide how or whether to formalize their relationship with the child in their care. In cases in which parents are completely out of the picture, or where their influence and involvement needs to be minimized, a strong case may be made for adoption. In cases in which the parental relationship exists, even if it is erratic and strained, there may be good reason to avoid the final step of adoption. If the child is older, seeking legal guardianship may be the best choice. In adoption, biological parents must either consent to the adoption or have their rights terminated in a court of law. Termination, if it is opposed by the biological parents, can take up to several years to accomplish. Still, it may be the best option in some situations. Legal guardianship can be a more temporary arrangement, leaving open the possibility that a parent who turns their life around may eventually be able to parent their child successfully.

Each family is different and what works for one may be a poor choice for another, even where the outward circumstances are the same. It is imperative that relatives considering adoption obtain quality help in reviewing their options and support in carrying out their decision. Because the boom in relative caregivers is recent, adoption and social work professionals may have little training and experience in advising them.

4. Deciding to adopt

Only you are in a position to decide whether adoption is right for you. You may obtain help from grandparent support groups. Consult those who have adopted, who have become legal guardians, or who have made other choices. Some relatives have decided their best option was to place the child with non-relative adopters in an open arrangement, allowing for continued contact.

Before exploring legal issues, explore the emotional ones. Support groups can help you locate experienced counselors; some have counseling staff. If the child has been in the custody of a public adoption agency, they may be able to direct you to counseling and support services. Look at the pros and cons of adoption and guardianship. Ask yourself what the consequences of a particular decision are likely to be. For example, if you choose adoption, your child's status and yours will be completely clear. You will be entitled to make the decisions that any parent is entitled to make. On the other hand, the adoption may come between you and the child's parents and disrupt what is left of the child's relationship with them. It may help to list the advantages and disadvantages of possible options. Ask what the purpose of adoption is in this case, and if there is any other way this purpose can be served short of adoption. And ask what the child's wishes are and what will happen to the child under each option. Finally, if the parents oppose adoption, what purpose, if any, would a legal battle serve? Whatever you decide, you are most likely to make a good decision if you call on all available resources to help you make it. If the children are old enough, their consent will be needed and, in any event, they should be involved in the process.

b. LEGAL REQUIREMENTS

The legal requirements for relative adoption, as for stepparent adoption, are usually less stringent than for non-relative adoptions. Relatives who wish to adopt may be given preference over non-relatives or non-relative foster parents. The Indian Child Welfare Act requires that before any non-relative is considered to adopt or foster a Native American child, adopters must be sought from the child's extended family.

If a child is sent from the custody of a parent, stepparent, grandparent, adult sibling, adult aunt or uncle in one state to the custody of one of the above in another state, the Interstate Compact on Placement of Children does not apply. Overall, many procedural requirements are relaxed for relative adoptions.

c. WORKING WITH A LAWYER

Since relative adoption, even where everyone supports it, can be an emotionally stressful experience, I recommend that you find a lawyer who is experienced in relative adoption, if possible, and in family law. Family practitioners are used to

185

dealing with clients undergoing emotional stress and many can direct you to counseling and other support services.

If you have become a custodial caregiver through the intervention and request of a public adoption agency or if you are the child's licensed foster parent, you may be able to have a lawyer from the agency advise and represent you in your adoption proceedings. If the agency feels that adoption is in the child's best interests, they may carry out the adoption for you. Be sure that you also receive advice on other options, such as legal guardianship. Some relative caregivers report that they have been pressured to adopt when they were far from certain it was in the child's best interests.

d. WORKING WITHOUT A LAWYER

This approach isn't for everyone. Doing your own adoption can be empowering if you feel up to it. It will also save you money. But it can just as easily add to the stress in your life. If you are already juggling social services, adjusting to the demands of new parenting responsibilities and family upheaval, the last thing you need may be trying to adopt on your own. Make sure you aren't eligible for free representation through your public agency before you take on this task. See chapter 9 for further information.

The proliferation of grandparent support groups means that there is almost certainly one in or close to your community. Throughout the process of adoption decision-making, relative caregivers should establish and maintain contact with such groups. Even if you are not a grandparent, they may be able to help you and offer support. Some have connections to social or other services, others are purely support groups. Ask for advice on decision-making, finding legal resources, references for attorneys, and pro se adoption. To locate a group in your community, contact the Brookdale Project listed in the Resource Guide. You could also call your local public adoption agency or foster family association.

RESOURCE GUIDE

1. Books and publications on grandparenting

Aldrich, Robert A., M.D. and Glen Austin, M.D. *Grandparenting for the 90s: Parenting is Forever.* Incline Village, NV: Robert Erdman Publishing, 1992.

Minkler, Meredith and Kathleen M. Roe. *Grandmothers as Caregivers: Raising Children of the Crack Cocaine Epidemic.* Newbury Park, CA: Sage Publications Inc., 1993.

Kids 'n' Kin: A Handbook for Relative Caregivers. Philadelphia Society for Services to Children's Support Center for Child Advocates. 1991

This excellent guide for relative caregivers offers information, advice, and solutions to common problems, including accessing financial support and services and dealing with the court system. It can be ordered from:

- The Philadelphia Society
  415 South 15th Street
  Philadelphia, PA 19146
  (215) 875-3400

2. Resources for relative adopters

- Brookdale Grandparent Caregiver Information Project
  Center on Aging
  140 Warren Hall
  University of California
  Berkeley, CA 94720
  (510) 643-6427; FAX (510) 642-1197

This project has been tracking grandparent caregiver support groups across the United States. So far, the project has learned of over 300 such groups, most of which offer support, services, referrals to services, and many of which have ties to health or social service agencies. The project publishes a newsletter, and it can help you identify support groups in your area and offer suggestions for how to start one.

TIPS

If you are uncertain on whether to become a foster parent or what the pros and cons are, contact the National Foster Parents Association (address given in the chapter 5 Resource Guide) for information on relative caregivers who have become foster parents. A high percentage of licensed foster parents began as relative caregivers. They can also discuss the pros and cons of adoption from the caregiver's viewpoint.

11

HOW CANADIANS CAN ADOPT IN AND THROUGH THE UNITED STATES

The United States and Canada share the world's longest unde-
fended border and citizens of both countries can cross it without
passport or visa. Because we have a common language and, to
some extent, a common culture, adopting a child born in one
country and bringing it into the other may seem more like
domestic than international adoption. In fact such adoptions are
every bit as "international" as adoptions of children born in
China or Peru. Many of the issues of race and culture examined
earlier apply to U.S.-born children brought to Canada.

a. SPECIAL CONSIDERATIONS

Every year, Canadian families adopt U.S.- born children and
bring them into Canada. Adoptions may be conducted
through an agency or independently facilitated. Further,
some U.S. agencies and facilitators help Canadian families
adopt children born in other countries. Neither the United
States nor Canada keeps statistics on how many Canadians
adopt U.S.-born children, but many adoption professionals
believe that numbers are growing. Because the states and
provinces have jurisdiction over adoption, neither federal
government oversees adoptions between the two countries,
apart from establishing and enforcing immigration laws.

Why should the U.S., which conducts the highest number
of international adoptions itself be placing children in homes
outside the United States? Aren't there American families for
these children? The answer to this question is complex. First,
Canadians who adopt newborns independently in the United

States are usually selected by birth parents from a number of potential adoptive families, most of whom are Americans. But if the Canadian family is preferred by birth parents, they will be chosen over an American family.

In the case of U.S. agencies, the issue of race is a strong factor in placement decisions. Most healthy infants available through U.S. agencies are African American or biracial. Some white U.S. adopters feel unable or unwilling to parent children of color. Others who are may feel that because some in the African American community oppose transracial placement, this option is closed to them. These adopters may conduct transracial international adoptions instead. For their part, agencies say that although efforts are made to find minority parents for U.S.-born children of color, they have more such children than families to adopt them. Consequently, agencies welcome applications from Canadian families and may even advertise in Canada for families.

b. OPTIONS FOR CANADIANS SEEKING TO ADOPT IN THE UNITED STATES

While all of the options below exist for some Canadians, they are not available in every province. Additionally, some U.S. state laws impose restrictions, such as residency requirements for adoptive families, which further restrict options.

1. Independent (private) adoption of U.S.-born children

With the help of a facilitator, a Canadian family is put in contact with birth parents and, after the birth of the child, the signing of consents, and any other legal requirements are observed, the family receives custody of the child in the United States. Thereafter, the adoption may proceed in either the United States or Canada, depending on the laws of the state and province involved.

2. Agency adoption of a U.S.- born child

In this case, a Canadian family applies to a U.S. agency and, if accepted into a program, is referred a child. The family travels to the U.S. to receive custody of the child and either concludes the adoption there or brings the child into Canada for adoption.

3. Adoption of a child born in third country, with the help of a U.S. intermediary or agency

A number of agencies and intermediaries in the United States help Canadians to adopt from third countries such as Uganda or Peru. In these cases, U.S. laws do not apply to the adoption, only the laws of the source country and Canada. However, the agency or intermediary may be licensed in the United States and services it provides will be governed by the laws of the state where it is licensed.

c. ADVANTAGES AND DISADVANTAGES OF U.S. FACILITATED ADOPTIONS

1. Advantages

(a) The U.S. is ten times larger than Canada and more children per capita are available for adoption. Choice and opportunities for adoption are greater than in Canada.

(b) Waits for newborns are often shorter than in Canada.

(c) For a Canadian minority family, especially of African or Native Canadian descent, options are greater for parenting a same-race infant and fees may be waived or relaxed.

(d) Private as well as public agencies are licensed in each U.S. state. There are a greater number of adoption professionals available to facilitate independent adoptions.

190

(e) There may be more flexibility in the U.S. (depending on the state and agency or facilitator) as to who is eligible to parent a child.

2. Disadvantages

(a) It is hard to imagine a process requiring more government involvement than a Canadian-U.S. adoption. At a minimum, Canadians must obtain the approval of their province, their federal government, and the state government where the child is born and/or adopted. In the case of an adoption involving two states, the laws of both states as mediated by the Interstate Compact on the Placement of Children will apply.

(b) A U.S. adoption may be more expensive than the Canadian equivalent.

(c) If the agency, facilitator, or birth parents, intentionally or not, commit an illegal or negligent act or go out of business, there may be no or only limited redress available to Canadian families.

(d) Many in the U.S. know little about Canada, its political and social history and demographics. It may be difficult to obtain quality counseling on issues such as whether transracial placement is an appropriate choice for a particular family.

(e) The Hague Convention on Intercountry Adoption will eventually apply to these adoptions. While it might make adoptions easier, it may just as easily result in a more time-consuming, costly, and difficult process.

d. WHICH OPTION IS RIGHT FOR YOUR FAMILY?

Review the options discussed in chapters 5, 7, and 8. All are applicable to Canadians. Any means of verifying the bona fides of a U.S.-based agency or facilitator can be accessed by Canadians.

For some Canadians, U.S. options may be limited. In Manitoba, independent international adoption is not available. Unless an agency is recognized in the province and/or is approved by the National Adoption Desk (NAD), international agency adoption is not available either. NAD does not currently have a U.S.-based program, although one may come into existence in the future. In some provinces the wait for an international home study can be years long.

e. STEPS TO AN ETHICAL ADOPTION

1. Gather information

Research available options and talk to parents who have adopted from the United States. The free AFA guide listed at the end of chapter 7 is a good place to begin looking for agencies. Other good resources are *Adoption Helper* (see the Resource Guide), the NAIC National Adoption Directory, *Loving Journeys,* which notes agencies and lawyers who place across the United States, and the *ICCC Handbook* which lists agencies which place with Canadian families.

The NAIC matrix of adoption laws can show you which states do not impose residency requirements for adoption. If you are considering independent adoption, be sure you are looking at states that allow it. States that prescribe a long wait between placing a child with adopters and finalization may be a poor choice. In such a case you will either have to place the child in some form of foster care for months, or bring the child into Canada on a minister's permit, which has many limitations.

2. Decide between agency and independent adoption

If you choose an agency, you are almost certainly going to be adopting transracially. Before choosing an agency, verify with your ministry responsible for adoption or with the National Adoption Desk in Ottawa that the agency is acceptable to them. Ask if they have any information about a source you are thinking of working with.

For Canadian families, agency adoption may be faster than independent adoption, especially if you are older adopters. Since most agencies place infants they have difficulty placing in the United States, competition will not be as stiff as for healthy Caucasian newborns who are greatly sought after in both countries. Agency adoption is more likely to result in a successful permanent placement than independent adoption in which birth parent rights may not be so easily resolved.

3. Interview sources

In addition to the questions listed in chapters 7 and 8, here are some more to ask that are specific to Canadian adopters.

(a) Have you facilitated an adoption or placed a child with a Canadian family before? From our province?

(b) If the answer is yes to either question, can you give us references to one or more Canadian adoptive families?

(c) If the answer is no, are you certain that state law allows Canadian families to adopt there or to bring a child into Canada for adoption?

(d) Do you or your state have any requirements for the adoptive home study that we need to be aware of? (For example, must it be done only by a licensed agency or may it be done by an independent social worker? Since the wait for provincial adoption agency home studies through the ministry responsible for adoption can be years long in some provinces, you need to be certain that an alternative acceptable to your U.S. source exists.)

(e) Are you familiar with the Canadian legal process for obtaining permanent residency and/or a minister's permit for our child? Can you help us through it? (While it is not necessary to have a source who is up to date on Canadian law to adopt through the United States, such agencies and facilitators do exist and they may be able to make your adoption speedier, more affordable, and hassle-free.)

4. Obtain and check references

Call the state adoption specialist for the state the source is licensed in. If you are using an attorney or facilitation service, check with the state bar association and the adoption specialist. Call AFA and ask if they have any information on the source. You can also contact your provincial ministry with jurisdiction over adoption, as well as the Adoption Council of Canada, NAD, Adoption Helper and any provincial or local adoptive parent association. Check out your source in both countries. An agency or facilitator may do a fine job of domestic adoption, but be less than adequate when placing children with non-U.S. families.

5. Select your agency or facilitator

If possible, make a preliminary application to your source in the United States before you arrange for a home study in your province. Be sure your source has accepted you as clients to adopt a child and verify what requirements, if any, they have for the contents of the home study. Then you can be sure that those issues are included in your provincial home study.

f. THE PROCESS

Independent adopters should adopt only with the help of an experienced facilitator, either a lawyer or a licensed facilitator who can refer you to a lawyer to ensure that legal requirements of all jurisdictions are met. It is best to work with a facilitator who takes full responsibility for finding birth parents since it would be difficult for a Canadian family to advertise and locate U.S. birth parents from Canada.

After you have chosen your source, you will need to arrange a home study. Whether you are adopting in the United States or in Canada, your home study must be done in Canada. Check with your ministry for social services and follow any guidelines. If your home study is valid for your province and for Canadian immigration purposes, it will usually be acceptable in the United States. However, you should always verify this.

Once you are accepted into an agency program, or have made an adoption plan through a facilitator, and have started (or completed) your home study, you will need to obtain and fill out a sponsorship form (called an Undertaking of Assistance) from your nearest Employment and Immigration office. After you have filed this, the usual practice is for Employment and Immigration to seek a Letter of Non-Involvement or Non-Objection from your provincial ministry in charge of adoption. This letter states that they are aware of your adoption plans and have no objection to them. Before issuing such a letter, each province's ministry may have requirements which must be met, such as a completed adoptive family home study.

When the Undertaking and Letter have been processed by Immigration, they will be sent to the closest of the four Canadian consulates in the United States with authority to issue immigrant visas. These are located in Buffalo and New York City in New York State; Seattle, Washington; and Los Angeles, California. As of the fall of 1993, these are the only Canadian consulates in the United States with such authority.

In addition to any documents, originals or copies, needed for Canada, you will need others for the U.S. part of your adoption. Verify with your U.S. source what documents they need in what form (i.e., notarized home study).

After you have submitted your home study and any supporting documents required by your source, you will be ready for a referral. Most Canadians adopting through the United States report that they waited less than a year, sometimes as little as six weeks. Some Canadians have received referrals so quickly that they have had to seek Immigration approvals, home study, and arrange for the care of their new child simultaneously. If you can ensure that your immigration file is complete by the time you are ready to take custody of your child, you will have an easier and less frantic time bringing your child into Canada.

Once you have received legal custody of your child in the United States, either through a facilitated or agency placement, you have two options for bringing your child into Canada: getting permanent residency status or using a minister's permit.

1. Permanent residency status

To obtain permanent residency status for your child on entering Canada, your adoption usually must be finalized in the United States. In some states, it may be possible for Canadians to travel to the United States, adopt, and return to Canada in one trip. If so, after your source has finalized the adoption in court, you should be able to obtain a U.S. passport for your child and then apply from one of the four Canadian consulates for an immigrant visa. During the wait for the passport, you can obtain the required medical exam for your child which is part of the Canadian visa application process. Employment and Immigration has specific requirements for who is to carry out the medical exam and what it consists of, so you will need to verify the procedures with them first.

Should your child fail the medical exam, or in the case of any procedural problems or delays with the adoption, you will need to obtain a minister's permit to bring your child with you into Canada and reside there until returning to the United States to finalize the adoption. In either case, obtain a U.S. passport for your child if possible. With your child's passport and immigrant visa allowing permanent residency status, you should be able to enter Canada as a family and complete the naturalization process there.

2. Minister's permit

If you are returning to and residing in Canada between receiving temporary guardianship of your child and finalization of the adoption, or adopting your child in Canada, you will need to obtain a minister's permit to bring your child into the country. To obtain one, you may apply to one of the four consulates listed above. Since Canadian missions in the United States are undergoing major changes, you should verify procedures with Employment and Immigration before leaving Canada.

To issue a minister's permit, Immigration must find that there are "compelling humanitarian and compassionate" factors to take into consideration. Generally speaking, a legal adoption by a Canadian family, completed in the United States between temporary guardianship and finalization in either country, or an adoption to be carried out in Canada, is construed as meeting this test.

A minister's permit is issued for a limited period of up to one year. If the child has not been granted permanent residency status by that time, an extension can be sought. There are two kinds of permit. One allows the holder merely to stay in Canada. In that case, the holder cannot leave Canada and re-enter at will until permanent residency status is obtained. The other kind of permit allows the holder to come and go as well as reside in Canada. Adoptive families holding this kind of permit should be able to travel out of Canada and return safely with the child. To do so, however, it is best to have a U.S. passport for your child. While travel to the United States should not be problematic, it could prove difficult to travel to any country that requires visas for entry. Most adoptive families whose children hold a minister's permit choose not to travel outside the country until permanent residency status is obtained.

If you have a choice, it is preferable to obtain your child an immigrant visa and permanent residency status than seek to enter Canada with a minister's permit. One important reason is health care coverage. Permit holders are often not covered by provincial medical plans. Medical coverage requires a private policy that can be fairly costly and may not cover as much as the provincial medical plan and are likely to refuse to pay for "pre-existing conditions," any medical problems originating prior to coverage. Because infants need frequent immunizations and checkups, raising a baby for a year or more without medical coverage or with a separate policy can be expensive.

g. NATIVE CANADIAN ADOPTERS

The U.S. Indian Child Welfare Act provides that after extended family, followed by tribal members, "Indian families" are next in line to adopt Native American children. While this has not been litigated, it would seem that Canadians who can prove that they are Indians (i.e., have tribal affiliation) may be able to adopt Native American infants in accordance with ICWA. If you are a Native family seeking such a child, you might contact tribes or adoption agencies in states with a large Native population, such as Alaska, Washington, New Mexico, or Montana.

h. AFRICAN CANADIANS

If you are of part or full African heritage, you should be able to adopt a similar infant easily through a U.S. agency. If agency fees are too high for your family, be sure to ask for a waiver or subsidy. United States agencies are under pressure to find minority homes for minority children where possible and most will bend over backwards to accommodate such a family which has been favorably recommended in a home study.

i. THE INTERSTATE COMPACT ON PLACEMENT OF CHILDREN

A little known fact about the ICPC is that it was passed so as to allow for participation by any and every Canadian province, should they choose to be included. All that is necessary is for the U.S. Congress to consent to a province's passage of the Compact into law. In that case, an adoption between that province and a U.S. state would proceed in accordance with the Compact just as an interstate adoption does now. The immigration process would need to be adjusted to accord with the Compact. However, the ICPC does hold promise, especially in light of the Hague Convention. Eventually, U.S.-Canadian adoptions will need to follow Convention guidelines. The ICPC may provide a structure through which the Convention could be implemented.

RESOURCE GUIDE

1. General

- Adoption Council of Canada
  P.O. Box 8442
  Station "T"
  Ottawa, Ontario
  K1G 3H8
  (613) 235-1566

2. Adoption publications

- *Adoption Helper*
  189 Springdale Boulevard
  Toronto, Ontario
  M4C 1Z6

This is Canada's only nationwide adoption periodical. Like *Ours*, it serves the adoption community and keeps readers informed on adoption issues. It publishes frequently updated adoption data sheets on different countries and each issue contains timely information on current adoption practices worldwide. American readers take note: this is the best periodical source for such information.

Bagnall, Kenneth. *The Little Immigrants: The Orphans Who Came to Canada*. Toronto, Ontario: Macmillan Press, 1980.

Bowen, John. *A Canadian Guide to International Adoptions*. Vancouver, BC: Self-Counsel Press, 1992.

Daly, Kerry S. and Michael P. Sobol. *Adoption in Canada*. Guelph, Ontario, 1993.

Every Canadian adoptive family should take a look at this report, the first in-depth report on adoption Canada-wide. The result of a 3-year study, the report found that there were three international for every two domestic adoptions in Canada in 1991. Copies of the report are limited. Planned Parenthood offices may have copies, as may adoptive parent groups, public, and university libraries.

- *Transition*
  Vanier Institute of the Family
  120 Holland Avenue, Suite 300
  Ottawa, Ontario
  K1Y 0X6
  (613) 722-4007

This bilingual periodical covers issues of importance to Canadian families, including adoption, foster care, education, new reproductive technologies, and economic issues.

TIPS

Below are some U.S. adoption agencies that place with Canadian families. While I have avoided listing particular agencies in this book, because they come and go quickly, the agencies below have been in existence for years and have a track record placing children with Canadian families. Other good agencies exist, so don't confine your investigation to these. Note that several are close to one of the Canadian consulates that can issue immigrant visas.

- Adoption Services of WACAP
  P.O. Box 88948
  Seattle, WA 98138
  (206) 575-4550

- Americans for African Adoptions Inc.*
  8910 Timberwood Drive
  Indianapolis, IN 46234-1952
  (317) 271-4567 (also FAX)

- New Hope Child & Family Agency
  2611 N.E. 125th, Suite 146
  Seattle, WA 98125
  (206) 363-1800

- The Open Door Adoption Agency Inc.
  116 East Monroe Street
  P.O. Box 4
  Thomasville, GA 31799-0004
  (912) 228-6339; FAX (912) 228-4726

- The Option of Adoption
  504 East Haines Street
  Philadelphia, PA 19144
  (215) 843-4343; FAX (215) 843-8681

---

*Places children born in Africa in U.S. and Canadian homes.

12
IMPLEMENTING YOUR STRATEGY

a. PUTTING IT ALL TOGETHER

Collecting documents, getting them stamped, sealed, and delivered; arranging time off from work; deciding whether and when to tell family and friends; preparing children in the family for the new child and planning the adoption itself: this chapter addresses these issues and how to develop a strategy for dealing with them once the adoption is under way.

b. FINANCIAL PLANNING

1. Adoption costs are a market phenomenon

Adoption fees are volatile. Agency and attorney fees have risen steadily. Medical care for birth mothers is subject to the same meteoric increases as it is for everyone else. If you adopt independently, you may have some control over costs. You can shop around for different services separately. Still, much of the process is beyond adopter control. For independent international adoption, costs are probably the most market-driven of all as well as least subject to legal and social controls. Facilitators have been known to bargain with various adopters to obtain the highest fee.

2. Cost increases in adoption

There is no standard practice with respect to fee hikes in adoption. Some agencies seem to raise fees annually, while others go many years without changing fees. Fee increases in increments of 30% to 50% are not unknown. It is important to budget for possible fee hikes when planning an adoption. At the same time, verify that after agreeing to a fee in writing you will not be expected to cover a further increase. Because some agency adoptions take years to accomplish, an agency may not ask you to pay a placement fee until the child is referred to you. The fee may be what is current then, not what the fee would have been at the time you were placed on a waiting list for a child.

When you are planning your finances for an agency adoption, investigate past fee increases there. Do they seem to raise fees each year? By how much? If they haven't raised fees for a long time, ask if a fee increase is likely to happen soon and if it could affect you.

In an international adoption, you should come to an agreement in writing about what your fee will be in advance. Ethical facilitators will stick to an agreement; however, some factors may be beyond their or your control. If a new legal process is instituted that affects adoption, more work may be involved for the attorney. Court filing fees can change. If the country is undergoing economic upheaval, the cost of caring for the child can rise. Modest additional payments may be justified. If, however, you are told your fee is to be doubled, that you should remit an unplanned for large payment, or that you must pay the entire fee in advance, you need to rethink the adoption.

3. Strategies for creative financing

For many, financing an adoption is a struggle. Because so many factors are beyond anyone's control and because the need for payment may arise suddenly, it is hard to plan in advance. But there are things you can do.

(a) Look for agencies that place with lower income adopters.

(b) Shop around for each service you need.

(c) Ask if the fee is refundable. A high refundable placement fee may be a better choice than a lower, non-refundable fee.

(d) Talk to other adoptive parents — they may give you ideas.

(e) Research all subsidy and support options.

(f) Plan a contingency budget. Try to reserve a sum equal to 25% of your adoption budget for emergencies.

c. PLANNING TIME OFF AROUND ADOPTION

1. Family leave

The newly passed Family Leave Act, discussed in chapter 2, allows adopters who work for the U.S. federal government or companies with more than 50 employees up to 12 weeks of unpaid leave per year to adopt. Time can be taken off to conduct the adoption and/or to spend with the child after placement.

For employees not covered by the act, getting sufficient time off to adopt can be difficult. You need to decide how much leave you must have and then consider how much you'd like on top of that. If you are a two working parent family adopting a domestic infant in-state, where one parent will stay at home with the baby after adoption, no more time may be needed than to attend the court hearings and a week or two more to bond with the new child.

If these two parents are adopting internationally, however, planning leave will be more challenging. International adoptions which require parents to travel rarely take less than two weeks. In some cases, two trips of a week to two weeks each are required, usually several months apart. In some countries, it is impossible to tell in advance how long you will have to stay. To get an idea of what's involved, talk to as many adopters as you can find who recently adopted from the same source.

In countries with government-regulated adoption, estimates are likely to be accurate. Where adoption is less regulated, estimates may be vague. If you are adopting from such a country, at least one parent needs to be able to add a week or even a month to a stay on short notice, to guarantee that the adoption can be completed. Families where such flexibility is impossible should choose another adoption route. Too many sad stories are heard of families returning home without a child only because they could not stay away from home any longer without losing their jobs.

2. Negotiating with employers for time off

Find out if your employer has an adoption leave policy. If you are covered by the Family Leave Act, make sure that the policy complies with the act. You can obtain a copy of the regulations (rules for implementation) of the act by calling or writing the nearest federal government bookstore.

Even if you are not covered by the act, your employer may have an adoption policy. If there is none, does your employer have a maternity leave policy? Do they treat the two kinds of parents the same or at least fairly?

A maternity leave policy may or may not be a good model for adopters to follow. You may need to apply much of any available leave toward the adoption process itself, which could leave little or no time to be with your child after placement. If you are adopting a special needs child, time after placement can be especially important. Arranging for medical or educational assessment and treatment is time-consuming. Being a new parent of any child is draining. A child who speaks no English, or a baby who has slept only in a hammock and eaten a totally different diet will require a considerable investment of parental time, energy, and creativity.

Even if the federal act doesn't apply, your state may have laws governing maternity and adoption leave which do. Call your state department responsible for employment practices and ask them to give or send you information on such laws. Before you try to negotiate with your employer, be sure you understand any applicable state and federal laws. Not all employers are aware of what the law is themselves. Don't expect them to alert you to your rights.

If your employer is reluctant to grant you flexible adoption leave, you need to recognize your employer's needs and concerns and be prepared to address them. The facts of adoption are not well-understood in our society. Employers may think that adopting is simple, predictable, and requires no special recovery time, since the mother isn't actually giving birth. The difficulties, unpredictability of the process, and the fact that bonding with a child is at least as challenging for adopters as it is for biological parents, may be news to many employers. Schedule time to talk to your employer and any other decision-maker and be prepared to educate them on adoption issues.

If you are a two-parent family, you may be able to divide leave between you so that one takes, for example, six weeks off and the other partner takes another six. Three weeks might overlap giving you, collectively, nine weeks full time with the child. Where an international adoption requires two trips or one extended trip, you may be able to arrange for one parent to remain or return home early and go back to work. Find out if this is possible in the country involved, before discussing leave arrangements with your employer.

Through an adoptive parent group, newsletter, or magazine, you may be able to contact adopters whose employers are roughly similar in size and needs to yours and who offer adoption leave. If possible, talk with their employer yourself for details on how the plan works in practice. Ask if they would allow you to refer your employer to them for further information.

Don't put off the discussion with your employer. You need to give your employer time to cover your absence. If he or she is the sort who would treat you adversely because you are adopting, you are better off finding out now than when you have big adoption bills and a new child to support.

Telling an employer you are planning to adopt in advance of a referral gives you time to explore options for leave and make any necessary adjustments to your work schedule. An employer may be more flexible given sufficient time to plan. In any event, check to make sure what your own obligations are under any employment contract. Be sure you comply with any requirements to give your employer a minimum specified amount of notice before leaving to adopt.

Finally, if you decide together on adoption leave, ask your employer to sign a written agreement with you specifying the terms, and, of course, if your employer is generous, show your gratitude. You may make it easier for the next adoptive family to obtain leave.

d. STRATEGIES FOR BECOMING AND STAYING INFORMED

1. Networking

Networking is the process of consulting your peers. Talking with others who have undergone the same experiences can open up new possibilities. My adoption happened through networking, as have thousands of others. Networking can:

(a) Introduce you to people and services that can help you achieve your adoption objectives

(b) Give you important information about the adoption process

(c) Provide you with an assessment and critique of the people and services you need to evaluate in coming to a decision

(d) Be a source of emotional support

(e) Provide you and, eventually, your children, with a peer group

206

2. Joining a support group

Many benefits of adoptive parent groups have already been described. These groups are often consulted when changes of adoption law and policy are contemplated by government. They are likely to be the first and most accurate source of information about changes in international adoption, health concerns of adopted children, and consumer information about adoption services. Relative and stepparent support groups can also help.

3. Subscribing to adoption newsletters and periodicals

Adoption periodicals discuss adoption issues in depth. Many feature columns by counselors, child development experts, and adoption lawyers. Issues of concern to the adoption community, such as the adoptee search movement, get an in-depth hearing. There is no quicker way to discover the current realities and concerns of adoption. Reputable (and some not so reputable) adoption services advertise in adoption periodicals. Bibliographies of adoption materials on adoption can be found, along with ethnic dolls and toys and information on cultural activities of interest to adoptive families. For rural adopters, these periodicals serve as a support network and lifeline to the adoption community.

4. Attending workshops, classes, and adoption fairs

Many adoption agencies hold free meetings about their services that are open to the public. These offer facts about adoption and the agency itself. Hospitals may offer workshops, usually for a modest fee, on infertility, parenting, decision-making, and adoption. Child welfare agencies sometimes give workshops on topics like grandparent adoption. Some adoptive parent groups sponsor workshops on adoption issues. Recently, adoption fairs have been held at which a variety of adoption services come together to offer information to the public. To find out what classes and workshops are available in your community, contact an adoption support group or your public state agency.

5. Churches and ethnic/cultural organizations

Community-based churches often support adoptive families. They may be able to help with adoption financing. Some birth parents turn to their church for help in making an adoption plan, so your church may be a good networking resource for finding a child. Since adoption professionals and birth parents often prefer children to be parented by families of the same or similar background, ethnic and cultural organizations can be an important networking resource to locate children and support services within your community.

If you are adopting transracially, be aware of the growing interracial community that supports interracial families of all kinds. Since transracial adoption is controversial, you may benefit from joining organizations that actively support multiracial families. This can be especially helpful if you live in a small community or don't know many families like yours. See the Resource Guides for chapters 5 and 13 for additional resources.

e. TROUBLESHOOTING

1. Dealing with setbacks

Few adopters come through the process without experiencing setbacks. But just as biological mothers tend to forget the stresses and pains of labor, we tend to forget the pains of adoption once we become parents. So much of adoption is beyond our control and subject to sudden change that even the best prepared adopters are likely to encounter problems at times. Don't be too hard on yourself if some problems are inadvertently caused by you. Adoption requires thousands of tiny exacting steps, the wisdom of Solomon, and the patience of a saint. None of us can manage all of these all of the time.

2. When birth parents change their minds

Some adopters, especially those who have already brought the child home, oppose a birth parent's subsequent withdrawal of adoption consent, all too often with tragic consequences. The adopters may take legal action; but usually such actions fail and the baby returns eventually to the biological parents. The longer adopters have spent with the child, the harder it is to say goodbye.

I believe that withdrawal of consent to adoption by the birth parents is a decision that you should accept immediately, should it occur. Voluntary adoption, where birth parents choose placement rather than having their child removed from them by child protective authorities, is first and foremost the birth parents' decision. Only after their decision is made do we as adopters enter the picture. If they change their minds, so be it. The adopters may have better resources, parenting skills, and education, but that is never a sufficient reason for adoption.

If a birth father refuses consent after a birth mother has made an adoption plan with you, she, too, may withdraw consent, especially if the birth father intends to seek custody himself. The birth mother may prefer to parent the child herself if otherwise the father will raise the child or decide who can do so.

Even the best planned adoption can fall through. Adoption professionals don't like to dwell on aborted placements, so adopters are sometimes surprised to learn that over half of all birth parents decide against placement after making an adoption plan. Such decisions may occur after the child has been placed with the adoptive family. In some areas the number may be as high as 15%. Most birth mothers do not finally make up their minds to place or not place their child with adopters until after they have given birth.

It is important to understand that this major setback is a real possibility in any newborn voluntary placement, and to plan for it. It is probably best to wait to send adoption announcements until the child is placed in your home, all consents are given, and the time during which birth parents may withdraw consent at will has expired. This may mean that you don't officially confirm your parenthood until weeks or longer after placement. But consider the alternative. In *Dear Barbara/Dear Lynne*, co-author Barbara Shulgold describes how, after sending out baby announcements, she was faced with the heartbreaking task of notifying friends and family that the adoption had fallen through.

Strike a balance between hopefulness and caution. Prepare a room for the baby by all means, but wait to buy baby clothes. You may end up adopting a child a little older, or younger, or of a different gender than you first planned. You can explore baby stores, consignment shops, garage sales, talk to close friends about car seats, and read baby magazines without investing in a particular placement. See yourself as a parent, not the parent of Baby X, at least until Baby X is born and in your home for good. Address adoption announcements, but don't fill them out until your placement is secure.

3. When the adoptive family situation changes

Infertility treatment and the difficulties of adopting place stress on a relationship. Adopters, during the long wait, may confront illness, a death in the family, a need to move or change jobs, or the loss of a job. Depending on the stage of the process, such changes may require readjustment of adoption plans.

Probably the most difficult change as well as the most common is a separation or divorce from your spouse. If you were hoping to adopt from a country where a prior divorce or single parenting is unacceptable, the breakup of your marriage will obviously change your plans. Birth parents who wish their child to be raised in a two-parent family may rethink placing their child with you. New financial concerns may also arise.

210

If you find yourself in this situation, counseling from a professional experienced in adoption may help. You will face issues and decisions that are not identical to those of a biological family during a divorce. Most adoption professionals understand that adoptive couples are no more "permanent" than others in our society and there is no reason to think that a divorce will prevent you from adopting eventually. If you have already received the referral of a child, however, you will need to discuss the situation immediately with your agency or intermediary.

Agencies respond differently to divorce in an adoptive family. Some may no longer wish to place a child with you. But many will help you plan what steps to take if you want to continue with an adoption. They may put your adoption on hold for several months or refer you for counseling. Larger agencies deal with this situation more often than you might expect and have policies in place to deal with it. If your relationship is in trouble at the time of your home study, you can expect an astute agency worker to realize this and offer suggestions for addressing the situation.

4. When an agency turns you down after the home study

In agency adoptions, this rarely happens. Usually, adopters learn whether they meet basic eligibility criteria before a home study is even scheduled. But in independent adoption, a family may not have undergone a pre-screening process and, therefore, may not realize they are unlikely to be approved in a home study until it happens. Even in independent adoptions, however, it is unusual for adopters to be disqualified.

Should you be turned down, your first step is to find out why. Ask for a copy of the home study and talk to the worker who did it. Ask what you can do, if anything, to change his or her mind. If you arrive at an impasse, you have several options. You can appeal to the worker's supervisor and ask for reconsideration. You can investigate other sources for a home study. If you do, be honest about having been turned down elsewhere and the reason that was given before you invest in a new home study. It is possible that one worker will find you unacceptable parent material while another feels you can parent adequately.

Most agencies have an appeal process in place which you should ask about when you first interview them. It may be possible to take legal action against an agency that issues a negative home study. Such action would be expensive, time consuming, and could fail. You are more likely to succeed if the worker's decision is based on a subjective assessment of your parenting abilities than if it is based on a fact such as a prior conviction for armed robbery. Seek legal advice from an experienced adoption attorney before pursuing this option.

5. When an agency or facilitator goes out of business

This situation confronts all too many adopters. The best way to cope is by advance planning. Keep in frequent touch with your agency or facilitator throughout your adoption. If you wait months without receiving a referral this does not necessarily mean there is a problem. However, ask staff for explanations and updates on your case about once a month. If it appears that the wait for a referral is much longer than you were originally led to believe, find out why. You are entitled to a clear explanation. It may be that the country the agency places children from is changing its adoption law or it may be that your facilitator is on the verge of bankruptcy, or the agency is losing its license.

If you cannot get an acceptable explanation, seek an independent assessment. Call your state adoption specialist and express your concerns. Call AFA and other adoptive parent groups, tell your story, and ask if they can provide any information. Options are limited after an adoption service goes under, so try to be alert for signs of trouble before it happens. A consistent refusal to return calls or respond to mail is a red flag. Vague responses to questions that require concrete answers are a bad sign.

When a licensed agency has done your home study, it should be valid if the agency later goes out of business provided the agency was licensed at the time the home study was carried out. If the study was partially completed, you may be able to use it and any supplements such as family financial statements, references, and medical reports as the basis for a new home study elsewhere. Another agency may be willing to complete the home study for a lower fee if you give them access to the work completed so far.

If you paid money for services and the adoption agency or facilitator you paid goes out of business before providing them, you are a creditor and, if there is enough money, you should be reimbursed. If this occurs, call your state attorney general's department immediately for information on your options.

6. When the child isn't who you expected

You should feel free to say no to a referral if you don't feel it will work for you. Many adopters do so for all sorts of reasons and later go on to adopt successfully. When a second Brazilian birth mother decided against placing her child with us, we were offered a baby from Guatemala. After anguished soul searching we turned down the referral; we had "bonded" with Brazil and couldn't see ourselves parenting a child from anywhere else. It took another year, but we finally adopted our Brazilian baby.

7. When a court denies an adoption

It is very rare for an adoption to be disallowed unless necessary consents were not given or adoption laws were broken. If a court denies your adoption, you may be able to appeal the decision to a higher court. To explore this option further, consult an experienced adoption attorney.

213

f. THE WAITING GAME

1. Coping with stress

Adopting a child is stressful. If you are a veteran of infertility treatment, you will be an old hand at coping with this kind of stress, but if you are preferential adopters who already have children, the critical scrutiny you receive along with a lack of entitlement and a loss of privacy may come as a shock. So much of your life is suddenly out of your control; even the aspects that aren't must be referenced to the adoption. The end result is that everything feels out of control. Your husband is offered a promotion at his company's head office in Michigan, but you have started an independent adoption, which is illegal in Michigan. Now what? Your wife is accepted into medical school on the same day your agency refers you twin baby girls from Honduras. Or you want to quit your job to write science fiction full time. You are sure you can afford it, but how will it look on your home study?

Apart from doing the best you can for matters within your control, there is nothing you can do to prevent stress. Too many decisions are out of your hands. What you can do is to develop a strategy for coping. Don't add to your stress by foregoing vacations. If money is a problem, go camping, visit relatives, or take a modest trip close to home. One November, a year after we had started our adoption and still with no baby in sight, my husband, three-year-old son, and I took a sudden holiday to Mexico. We couldn't really afford it; we had been planning to save all my husband's vacation leave for the adoption, but we needed a break. It proved to be one of the best holidays we've ever had. It was a lot easier not to worry about our adoption on the beach at Puerto Vallarta than it had been in rainy Seattle. We recharged our batteries and restored our sanity, which we needed because it was another 14 months before our adoption came through.

214

2. To tell or not to tell

Whether to tell people about the adoption is a personal decision. There is no one right answer. Some of it is out of your hands. You will need to tell your employer and the people you use as references in your home study. Your doctor will need to know. In international adoption you may need references from a priest, minister, or rabbi, your bank manager or mortgage lender. With notaries, social workers, criminal background checks and fingerprints, it's easy to feel as if the entire world knows all about your adoption before you even have the referral of a child. In fact it is possible to keep adoption fairly confidential, within limits.

The advantages of telling people in advance are that you will gain emotional support from friends and family and you will also set up an informal network for yourself. You may find out, for example, that a coworker has a pregnant teenage niece looking for adoptive parents.

On the other hand, when people know you are adopting, they expect it to happen overnight. You can expect frequent questions such as "any news yet?" from anyone you have told while you wait — and wait — and wait. You will get well-intentioned advice from those who know little or nothing about adoption. Along with genuinely useful tips you will hear "I know someone who adopted from Romania four years ago. Why don't you try that?" You'll also get the not-so-kindly meant interference: "If you can't have one of your own, accept it as God's will" or "How can you be adopting a baby from Chile when there are so many children in our country who need families?"

Some of us feel uncomfortable coping with pity from those we are not close to. Many adopters have to face the collapse of at least one adoption plan and in the aftermath, listen to expressions of sympathy from everyone who knows the story. One way to avoid this is to tell coworkers and extended family about the adoption, but withhold particulars until the placement occurs.

3. Helping family and friends to understand

You may find to your surprise that even your nearest and dearest have very little sense of what you are going through in adopting. David Kirk in his research with adoptive families discovered that most had experienced insensitive and hurtful remarks or questions about adoption. Adopters today report that little has changed. Often unconscious, negative attitudes toward adoption are still common and not only you but your children and possibly your parents will encounter them. Learning how to respond and teaching your children how to do so is important.

Family and friends almost always want to be supportive. When they aren't, it's usually out of ignorance. Refer them to adoption books and periodicals. If they aren't readers, lend, buy, or rent them a video or audio tape about adoption. Bring them to an adoption workshop or support group gathering. When they say something hurtful, let them know how you feel and why as soon as possible.

g. GETTING READY — DOMESTIC ADOPTION CHECKLIST

Your home study is done and you have accepted the referral of a child or made an adoption plan with birth parents. Here is a checklist of things to do in planning for your child's arrival:

(a) Verify health coverage for your new child. If the child has special needs, work with your private or state agency to plan for health care assistance. If your child is not eligible for assistance, make sure you know how to activate your health insurance plan to cover your child.

216

(b) Choose a pediatrician or general practitioner. Interview doctors, nurses, and nurse practitioners. Seek out medical professionals with experience of adoptive families as patients and who have a positive attitude toward adoption.

(c) Make a will if you don't already have one. You will need to appoint a guardian to raise your child should you and your partner die. You can take steps to prepare a will now and simply add the name of your child once the adoption is concluded. If you are doing an independent adoption, your attorney may be able to prepare your will. Storefront legal offices offer simple will preparation services at affordable prices. If you feel up to the challenge, you can prepare your own will. Self-Counsel Press has publications on will preparation and California's Nolo Press offers guidebooks and computer software to help you draft your own will.

(d) Once you have children, a life insurance policy will help provide for them should you die. Term life insurance offers broad coverage at a low cost. If you already have insurance, you will need to amend it to include your child as a beneficiary.

(e) Take a parenting class. Hospitals offer classes along with community colleges and university extension programs. Videos on parenting can be a great resource: watching someone demonstrate different techniques for soothing a colicky baby can teach you more than reading an article. If you are adopting a special needs child your agency or a larger agency that places such children may offer classes and workshops. To locate local parenting resources, start with your state social services department or public adoption agency. For more ideas see the Resource Guide.

(f) Plan your own personal parenting education. Take time to select materials on child development that are comprehensive and support your parenting views.

(g) Prepare children already in your family for the new child. How you do this is a personal matter, but it is important to consider how the adoption will affect your children. Are you changing the birth order? Many families do so and are pleased with the results. Still, since most children don't acquire older siblings, preparation is needed. If you are adopting a special needs child, preparing your children will require further consideration. If you are adopting transracially, race-related issues will also need addressing. See the chapter 13 Resource Guide for books on introducing the new child into your family.

(h) Consider breastfeeding. It is usually possible to nurse an adopted infant, although the nurture provided is primarily emotional, not nutritional. Your local adoptive parent group may include someone who has nursed an adopted child and can help you prepare. See the Resource Guide for more information.

(i) Plan for your child's arrival. Don't overlook borrowing. Adoptive parents are often older than most new parents and our age-peers may have finished with their baby clothes and furniture and be looking for somewhere to store it. If your child has special needs, a support group of families of similar children, adopted or not, can offer advice on outfitting your child.

(j) Decide on a baby shower. Your friends and family may want to welcome your new child with a shower. If you have strong feelings about the matter and feel comfortable doing so you may wish to raise the topic yourself. Many adopters do not want a celebration until the child is in their home. Others are more than happy to mark the long wait with a shower. If birth parent rights are fully resolved, a shower before placement doesn't raise difficulties. But if you have made an adoption plan with a birth mother who has yet to give birth, remember that she may still decide against adoption. If that happens you will have to tell the friends who attended your shower that the placement has fallen through and you will have a collection of gifts as an unhappy reminder. Many adopters tell family and friends that they would love a shower — after the child is in their home and the adoption is final.

(k) Prepare and address adoption announcements. You might design your own or select one from among the advertisers in adoption periodicals. Many card shops carry adoption announcements. We prepared our own custom-made announcements in which we identified and thanked everyone (over 50 people) who helped us adopt our daughter. This kind of announcement can serve to educate friends and family as to the enormous investment of time, money, and human resources that go into an adoption. I can guarantee that no one who read our adoption announcement will ever say "you did it the easy way" to an adoptive parent!

(l) Locate community resources if you are adopting an older, special needs child. If your child is in a wheelchair, which community swimming pools have swim times for wheelchair users? If your child is likely to need special education services, how will you secure them? Make an appointment to talk with teachers and administrators. Find out what education program choices are available to you and talk to parents with children in them. If you are adopting transracially, what can your community offer to your now multiracial family?

(m) Celebrate. Recognize that after your adoption your life will change forever. Celebrate and mourn the passing of your old life. Make your own ceremony.

h. GETTING READY — INTERNATIONAL ADOPTION CHECKLIST

You have accepted a referral of a child who is living in another country and are waiting for your paperwork to be processed and/or any necessary approvals such as INS advance processing. You know who your child is, how old and possibly have a photograph and a little biographical information. On the other hand, you may know nothing aside from the age, gender, and probable health status of your child. You are told you will be able to travel "soon," which could mean two weeks, two months or two years. Now what?

First, refer to the domestic checklist in section **g.** above. Most of those items apply to you, too.

(a) Obtain a passport if you don't have one. Renew an existing passport if it appears even remotely possible that it will expire within six months of the date you expect to return to North America. Many countries will not issue visas to people whose passports will expire within six months.

(b) Learn how to obtain a visa for the country you are adopting from. (Canadians do not need U.S. visas to enter the United States for the purpose of adopting.) Some countries issue tourist visas to adopters; others issue business visas. Contact the nearest consulate of the country you are adopting from and find out what documents they need to issue you a visa. Verify what the fee and the visa procedure is for any children in your family. If one of you is a naturalized citizen or doesn't have citizenship, tell the consulate. How long will it take them to issue the visa to you? Visas are usually stapled or stamped onto your passport so the consulate will need your passport when they issue the visa. Find out how you can get your visa to them safely. If you don't live within easy traveling distance of the consulate, compare prices of visa services and learn what their procedures are. You can obtain visa application forms at this stage, but don't fill them out until you have made your trip reservations. If you obtained the visa form a long time before you actually travel, check with the consulate that it is still the correct form, since they may now use a more recent one. Locate a photographer who takes visa pictures, but don't get them taken until just before you are ready to travel. Most countries have strict specifications for visa photos.

(c) Line up translators and interpreters, if necessary. If you are adopting in a sparsely populated, non-tourist community, verify before traveling what resources will help you communicate once you are in the country. While help should be provided for appointments and court hearings, locating assistance for the day-to-day business of caring for you and your child may be more difficult. Discuss this with your facilitator or agency. If you feel inadequate support is available; there are some often overlooked options to consider. Does the U.S. have a Peace Corps program there? If so, a volunteer posted nearby may be available to help you buy diapers, change airline tickets, or talk to a doctor. Another possibility is English-speaking missionaries who live in the community. The American Baptist Church and the Seventh Day Adventists, among many others, have a large missionary presence in many countries. These people can be terrific resources for adoptive families. Contact the Peace Corps or a church well before traveling.

(d) Draft and have translated a letter describing children already in your family. In many countries, child abduction is a problem, especially by non-custodial parents. If you are traveling with other children besides the adoptee, you should carry a notarized letter, translated into the local language, that describes this child

221

or children and add identification, such as a certified copy of the child's birth certificate, which proves the child is yours. It can save you untold hassles to be able to produce such a letter to airline and police officials.

(e) Investigate travel options. Which airlines fly to your child's country? Compare prices and services. Find out when the high (tourist) season is for the country. If it is in the southern hemisphere, the high season may be January and February. Does the country shut down for a major holiday? Does everyone go on vacation the same month? What happens to airfares then? Adoptive parents who have visited the country recently should be contacted. Several travel agencies specialize in serving adoptive families and advertise in adoption periodicals. An agency that specializes in travel to the country you are going to is also a good bet.

(f) Learn about health care, common diseases, and required and recommended vaccinations. Contact your local health department for information on health issues pertaining to the country. Some vaccinations must be given well in advance of travel. Those that are effective only for a short time should be left until you have travel dates. Learn which vaccinations are mandatory and which are merely recommended. Be sure that you know which is which; if not, you may face the prospect of being vaccinated overseas with a hypodermic needle whose origin you are not sure of.

(g) Read about the culture. Who are the country's great novelists, poets, and historians? Their books will be translated into English. Many public libraries have extensive video tape collections that include films from many countries. Check out the country's great film masterpieces along with travel videos. Read about the culture in newspapers and magazines. If you are unfamiliar with developing countries, read

222

about the Third World. See the Resource Guide for this and chapter 8 for further suggestions.

(h) Make arrangements to pay for your trip once you are in the country. Learn which credit cards are accepted and if U.S. and Canadian travelers' checks are easy to cash. If you don't have one, you may want to obtain a major credit card. If the currency is unstable and inflation is high, you will want to avoid paying in the country's currency whenever possible. Credit cards and travelers' checks can be replaced if lost or stolen. If you are going outside urban areas, learn how you will be expected to pay there. If you are in a small town with limited banking facilities, how will you pay for meals and hotels? When you evaluate accommodation and in-country travel be sure to find out in advance how they expect to be paid. A hotel that charges five dollars a day more may also accept travelers' checks.

(i) Plan an emergency fund. If you are robbed or find you must stay longer than you had planned, how can money be sent to you? Find out how you can transfer funds electronically to a bank abroad and make sure you have that option. Your own bank is a good place to start. You can also call the country's consulate and ask if there is a state bank which you can use.

(j) Choose parenting guidebooks. You will almost certainly be given custody of your child shortly after you arrive in the country. You may want to pick out an all-purpose text on infant and childhood development and health issues. If this will be your first child, read the book before you go, too. If the language of the country is unfamiliar to you, get a list of doctors and health facilities that offer service in English. (Good travel guides often include them.) The U.S. embassy there will have a list of doctors who speak English, too.

(k) Look into medical care options for yourself. If you get sick, how will you pay for treatment? If your policy doesn't cover you, consider buying travel health insurance. Health care is expensive in every country and a single doctor's visit may cost you $50.

(l) Learn something of the language. You might check out audio tapes from the library or read a do-it-yourself language workbook. The more you understand, the better time you'll have. Buy a good dictionary. If you are going to Latin America, make sure your dictionary is for that region. The Spanish and Portuguese spoken there differs greatly from that spoken in Europe. If you are adopting from a country with a very different alphabet or no alphabet at all, your task will be more challenging. The earlier you start the better.

(m) Decide whether to bring your children with you. Acquiring a new sibling is difficult enough for any child; acquiring one after a parent or parents have been away for weeks or months is a challenge for even the best adjusted. Even if you are going to a rural area where accommodation is rugged, drinking water is impure, and life is hard, you can bring your child with you. Yours will receive extra attention and you will find that many people will reach out to you as a family. We traveled with a very finicky four year old to the interior of one of the poorest, hottest states in Brazil and never for one instant regretted it. It is true that our son lived almost exclusively on grilled cheese sandwiches, crackers, and peanut butter and spent more time watching ninja turtle cartoons in Portuguese than we would have wished. But on the other hand, he was with us when we met our daughter and elicited her first chuckles. He charmed the hotel staff where we lived for three weeks and he was a walking advertisement — mostly good — for our parenting expertise.

(n) Pack for your new child. This is a challenge when you are planning for a child you've never seen in a country you've never visited for a stay of unknown length. If you are traveling with other children, the job is even harder. Here's a beginning:

- Sturdy, durable luggage

- Daypack (can double as a diaper bag)

- Baby carrier (a front pack if you are adopting a child under six months; otherwise a backpack)

- Clothing for you, any children you take with you, and for the child you are adopting. Bring only what can be laundered quickly and easily by hand. Laundromats are rare in many places. Research appropriate dress in the area, including for children. In a hot climate, natural fabrics like cotton are preferable to synthetics, especially for babies. If you have no information on your child's size pack for a child six months older and choose loose fitting items which can help protect against sunburn and insect bites.

- Medication and drugs (all prescriptions for as long a stay as your worst case scenario indicates)

- Baby medicine (discuss with your doctor. Include over-the-counter items like liquid acetaminophen and diaper rash skin cream. While these are available abroad, instructions for use will not be in English.)

- Electrical adapters (research which are required)

- Disposable diapers (available worldwide, but often costly and of poor quality)

- Diaper changing pad

- Baby wipes

- Feeding paraphernalia. For a child of up to two or who you know is bottle fed, bring only a few lightweight plastic bottles and nipples; your child may be firmly attached to a nipple available only in the birth country fitting only a bottle sold there. Bring bottle brushes and a gentle cleaning liquid such as Ivory. You may find yourself preparing baby formula with hard-to-dissolve powder. A fine strainer to get lumps out will save untold aggravation. If you will be preparing formula in your hotel room (and many do) bring something to boil water in — a small stove or heating coil. A lightweight, insulated bottle carrier is useful. Many adopters, out of sheer desperation, have discovered that a six-month-old child can be persuaded to enjoy cold formula.

A child of five months or older may be able to drink from a cup. A plastic no-spill cup with a secure lid handle, bowls, and easy-to-use child spoons are useful. You may find yourself opening baby food jars and serving dinner on a bus trip. Bibs are recommended. Bring along a good can and bottle opener. Twist-off lids are unknown in many countries.

- Toys (Age appropriate and easy-to-pack such as inflatable toys, nesting cups, cloth books, teething rings, nontoxic erasable pens and paper, tape player, earphones and children's tapes, straps with snaps at either end are great for attaching to a crib or high chair)

- Food for children you are bringing with you (a plastic jar of peanut butter or granola bars can ensure that even a finicky child will get some nourishment)

- Baby food and formula (only if you have first verified that no easy-to-prepare alternative exists in the child's country). Formula and baby foods similar to that sold in North America are available in much of the world. Your child will be accustomed to the local cuisine, so why add to the adjustments your child must make if you don't have to? Unless it's impractical or nutritionally deficient, consider continuing your child's diet as it has been until you return home. If that means baby food with added sugar and salt for a few weeks, so be it. There will be plenty of time to wean the child to the diet of your choice when you're home.

- Gifts (You will meet people who have played an important role in your adoption. While you should never offer a bribe or a gift of money, a thoughtful, inexpensive gift will be welcome and appreciated. Bring something typical of your community or which has some significance for you. We took packages of dried cranberries and wild rice with us, since both are unknown in tropical Brazil, and gave them out as hostess gifts. A book of photographs of your region is a good choice. Ask the agency, facilitator, or someone who comes from the country what gifts would be appreciated. Take along gifts for children, such as metal cars and trucks, hair bows, cute socks, troll dolls, or ninja turtles. They can be given to hotel staff, to foster family relatives, and to the adults and kids you are certain to encounter who go out of their way to help you.)

- Photo album. In many countries family ties are even more important than they are to us. Demonstrating that they matter to you, too, can help promote a positive image of adopters. You might include pictures of your extended family, your home — inside and out — and local sights of interest. We showed ours to many people, from our daughter's foster family to hotel and airline staff, judges and strangers on the bus. The album showed that we were a family like any other. Someone who speaks the language in your community may be willing to write photo captions for you. If you are adopting an older child, consider preparing a simple album as an introduction to his or her new home. You can make some real progress in preparing your child for new sights and pass some time in dreary hotel rooms and airports.

- Camera and film. (Consider adding a Polaroid camera, which can give people you meet an immediate memento of your visit. It's a great ice breaker. If you bring a video camera, remember that adoptions are usually confidential outside North America, too. As with domestic adoption, ask permission before taping any official proceeding.)

- Zip lock and other plastic bags of several sizes (in many countries paper and plastic bags are hard to find).

- Books (You may do a lot of waiting; books in English will be hard to find)

- Journal (to record your trip and start your child's lifebook)

- Tools (masking tape, all-purpose sink plug, heavy twine, scotch tape, scissors, flashlight and batteries, a good knife, bungee cords, padlocks, and keys for suitcases will all come in handy)

- Appliances (shortwave radio, travel alarm clock, pocket calculator)

- Money belt or pouch (for crime prevention)

Leave some room for children's books, tapes, and other keepsakes you buy or are given. Consult your travel guidebook for other suggestions. While this list may seem long, most items are relatively lightweight and easily packed. Leave yourself time for packing and you'll manage to fit everything in.

RESOURCE GUIDE

1. Financial planning

Dacyczyn, Ann. *The Tightwad Gazette: Promoting Thrift As A Viable Lifestyle.* New York: Villard Books, 1993.

2. Grief and loss

Levine, Stephen. *Guided Meditations, Explorations and Healings.* New York: Doubleday, 1991.

Stearns, Ann. *Living Through a Personal Crisis.* New York: Ballantine, 1991.

RESOLVE offers support to those who have lost children through miscarriage and aborted placements. See the chapter 4 Resource Guide.

3. Managing stress and change

Kabat-zinn, Jon. *Full Catastrophe Living: Using the Wisdom of Your Body and Mind to Face Stress, Pain, and Illness.* New York: Dell Publishing, 1990.

Wonder, Jacquelyn, and Priscilla Donovan. *The Flexibility Factor.* New York: Ballantine, 1989.

4. Helping others to understand

Bothun, Linda. *When Friends Ask About Adoption: A Question and Answer Guide for Non-Adoptive Parents and Other Caring Adults.* Chevy Chase, MD: Swan Publications, 1987.

Holmes, Pat. *Supporting an Adoption.* Wayne, PA: Our Child Press, 1986.

See also chapter 4 Resource Guide.

5. Choosing a health care provider

Williams, Stephen J. and Sandra J. Guerra. *Health Care Services in the 1990s: A Consumer's Guide.* New York: Praeger, 1991.

6. Life Insurance

Nader, Ralph and Wesley Smith. *Winning The Insurance Game.* New York: Doubleday, 1993.

7. Breastfeeding an adopted child

La Leche League International. *The Womanly Art of Breastfeeding.* New York: Plume, 1991

La Leche League International. *Nursing Your Adopted Baby.* Pamphlet 55.

This pamphlet can be ordered from La Leche League, P.O. Box 1209, Franklin Park, IL 60131-8209.

8. International development issues

Benjamin, Medea and Andrea Freedman. *Bridging the Global Gap: A Handbook to Linking Citizens of the First and Third Worlds.* Cabin John, MD: Seven Locks Press, 1990.

Brown, Lester, et al. *State of the World, 1993.* New York: Norton, 1993.

Ennew, Judith and Brian Milray. *The Next Generation.* Philadelphia, PA: New Society Publications. 1991.

Hamilton, John Maxwell. *Entangling Alliances: How the Third World Shapes Our Lives.* Cabin John, MD: Seven Locks Press, 1990.

Ramphael, Shridath. *Our Country, the Planet: Forging a Partnership for Survival.* Winnipeg, Manitoba: International Institute for Sustainable Development, 1992.

Tremblay, Helen. *Families of the World.* New York: Farrar, Strauss and Giroux, 1988.

9. Other resources on international issues

Call or write these organizations for their catalogues of publications.

- The American Forum for Global Education
  45 John Street, Suite 908
  New York, NY 10038
  (212) 732-8606

- Bread for the World Institute
  802 Rhode Island Avenue N.E.
  Washington, DC 20018

- Center for Teaching International Relations (CTIR)
  University of Denver
  Graduate School of International Studies
  Denver, CO 80208

- Network of Educators on the Americas (NECA)
  1118 — 22nd Street N.W.
  Washington, DC
  (202) 429-0137

- Pueblo to People
  2105 Silber Road, Suite 101- 49
  Houston, TX 77055
  1-800-843-5257

10. Health care for travelers

Schroeder, Dirk G. *Staying Healthy: In Asia, Africa, and Latin America.* Chico, CA: Moon Publications, Inc., 1993.

11. Traveling with children

Wheeler, Maureen. *Travel with children.* Berkeley, CA: Lonely Planet Publications, 1985.

(Out of print, but can be found in libraries and travel bookstores.)

TIPS

Most larger communities have foreign language instruction available through college and university extension programs, cultural exchanges, and with private tutors. Finding instruction for a language other than French or Spanish can be difficult. Your public library is a good place to start. Some libraries keep track of community language instruction resources.

Consider subscribing to periodicals that cover world news. To find them may require a little searching. Start with your public library, any college or university libraries, specialized bookstores, and newstands that carry a wide variety of periodicals. Community ethnic groups may have copies or know where they can be obtained. To get you started, look for the *Christian Science Monitor, The New Internationalist, Central America Report, World Monitor, World Press Review, World View* (published by the National Council of Retired Peace Corps Volunteers), and *World Watch.* A digest of news from periodicals around the world, *Subtext,* is available from 1408 - 18th Ave., Seattle, Washington 98122.

13
NOW YOU'RE A PARENT

Making the transition from would-be adopter to hands-on parent is quite a different process from bringing your biological child home from the hospital. This chapter looks at how you can move from the state of non-entitlement that we examined in chapter 1 to full-fledged parenthood.

a. FINDING NEW PARENT RESOURCES

Unlike pregnancy, the state of adopting is all-consuming. A pregnant woman has time and energy to consider baby names, buy baby clothes and furniture, and read books on child development, all with the comfortable knowledge that her baby will arrive within a set time frame — about eight months from the time her pregnancy is confirmed.

As we've seen, adopters have no such certainty during our "pregnancies." We have no way of knowing in advance how long our "gestation" will be and in any event we are so overwhelmed with home study, document preparation, and financing, that we scarcely have time to consider how will we feel as parents. Throughout an adoptive "gestation," adopters receive little positive reinforcement of themselves as parents. Because many in our society see adoption as second best or a form of charity, they react to hearing of an adoption without seeing the adopters as "normal" parents. Some of these effects are subtle, but when added together they can affect adopters profoundly. When the child is finally in their home, adopters must work harder than biological parents to feel accepted and competent in their new role.

232

Preferential adopters will not experience the same kind of discrimination. However, they may find that they are assumed to be adopting exclusively out of charitable motivation, not because they want to parent another child. Adopters of special needs children are often assumed to be very different indeed.

Grandparent adopters find their peer group is mostly a generation younger, with different cultural experiences and values. Stepparents, especially stepmothers without biological children, may be faced with a challenging parenting role and little if any social support. In all these situations, the task is the same: to become and feel competent as parents without receiving the same level of social acceptance as biological parents receive.

Adoptive parent groups, grandparent support groups, or stepfamily organizations, can help. If you are a minority-within-a-minority — a parent of a special needs child, disabled parent, homosexual, single parent, older parent, or of a minority race yourself — you may want to investigate support groups for that minority as well. Not only will you pick up valuable parenting tips, you will be in a group that affirms and reinforces your identity as a competent parent.

At the end of the chapter are listed some resources on raising adopted children. They discuss when and what to tell your child about the adoption, dealing with problems common in adoptees such as attention deficit/hyperactivity disorder, building your child's self-esteem, and dealing with prejudice. One resource which doesn't exist is an ordinary child development text that addresses adoptive parent issues side by side with those of biological parents. First-time adoptive parents of newborns need to know that most babies go through a fussy stage which peaks at around eight to twelve weeks of age. When your child development book assumes that the baby you are parenting is always your biological child, it doesn't attempt to allay your fears that a child's normal fussiness is actually separation anxiety caused by the adoption process. On the other hand, when your child exhibits a behavior that is likely caused or intensified by adoption, such as attachment disorder, no child development book will discuss it in that context.

If you have chosen medical professionals familiar with adoption issues, you should be able to rely on them for help in diagnosing adoption-related health problems or behaviors. Medical professionals inexperienced in treating adoptive families may fail to pick up cues that more knowledgeable professionals would notice. If you are dissatisfied with your communication with your child's health care team, discuss the issue with other adoptive parents. They may offer advice and suggestions. And discuss your concerns with the health care team directly. If you feel they lack the resources and training to treat your family adequately, and you cannot resolve the problem satisfactorily, choose a new team.

If you are an older, relative adopter, you might seek out biological and infertile adoptive families who are also older for support. Today an increasing number of parents are over 40. You may have more in common with them than with biological parents younger than your own children.

b. PARENTING ISSUES UNIQUE TO ADOPTION

Some issues are unique to adoption. While they affect every adoptive family, they are beyond the scope of biological parenting.

1. Telling your child about the adoption

Inform yourself about when and how to tell your children they were adopted. Adoption professionals do not agree about when to tell, but all agree that it should be done during childhood. In transracial adoption, you will be forced to deal with the issue earlier, since by the age of two your child will be well aware that you don't look alike. Even if your child was older and aware of the process when adopted, you will need to discuss adoption.

Your child is bound to have more questions that need addressing. Adoption professionals point out that just because a child doesn't raise the topic doesn't mean that they don't think about it a great deal. Each child development stage is different: concerns and anxieties of a three-year-old differ from those of a nine-year-old or a fourteen-year-old. To sensitize yourself to this topic, you could spend time with adult adoptees who are willing to answer questions about how they felt about their adoption growing up. Adoptive parent group workshops also frequently address when and how to discuss adoption with your children.

2. Finding your child a peer group

Every adopter, and especially transracial and non-traditional adopters, should make sure that their child has the opportunity to spend time with, preferably to grow up around, others in a similar situation. It's not enough to give your child books to read about adoption and race or hold occasional discussions on the issue. You probably considered how you would do this while preparing for your adoption and the question almost certainly came up during your home study and possibly your adoption hearing. Some adopters, however, find themselves so overwhelmed with parenting chores that it takes them years, if ever, to realize that their child needs to know they are not a one-of-a-kind being. To provide their child with a peer group, some families have moved into communities that are more ethnically diverse or that have more adoptive families. Adoptee support groups for adolescents and teenagers can help.

Across the continent adoptive family groups often sponsor summer culture camps and events that celebrate children's birth cultures. Culture camps may last one day or as long as a week and usually provide an intensive exploration of the music, food, dance, stories, games, and history of the pertinent country. Culture camps may cover several countries at once, such as

Latin American culture camps for children adopted throughout Central and South America.

Resist the temptation to trivialize the issues of culture and race. There is more to a culture than a few holiday celebrations, a "typical" dish, and a doll in native costume. Because of their availability, it is easy to focus exclusively on entertainment when we get involved in our child's culture. But there is more to a culture than recreation. Each country has a unique history, values, achievements, and tragedies. Learning about and keeping up with these is important in developing a true sense of what our child's culture is really about. By all means buy the dolls, books, and toys. But also consider subscribing to a reputable news source about the region such as those listed in the Resource Guide for chapter 12.

If you adopted transracially within the United States, these issues are equally important. Some white adopters are nervous about approaching the African American community because they have heard that many people there oppose transracial adoption. While not everyone in any race favors transracial adoption, adopters do have strong allies in interracial families. Over the past 20 years, transracial marriage has increased dramatically among all races in North America. These families have strongly supported transracial adoptive families and have joined together to advocate for recognition of interracial families. There are now many interracial support groups and at least three national periodicals in the United States alone targeted for multiracial families (see the Resource Guide).

3. Being alert for problems common to adoptees

Adoptees have a higher rate of attention deficit/hyperactivity disorder than the population at large. More adoptees need psychological counseling. Many older adoptees carry emotional scars which, sooner or later, require intervention. Some have disabilities to cope with as well as the adoption itself. Adoption periodicals often offer the latest medical research on adoptee issues. When medical or psychological research is being conducted on adoptive families, test participants are often solicited through adoption periodicals. You can keep your level of awareness of both problems and solutions high by reading adoption periodicals.

4. Developing realistic expectations for parenthood

Parenting is hard. Many adopters are dismayed to find they have days when they think back fondly to pre-parenting, and feel anything but lucky that they are — at last — parents. Some experience feelings similar to post-partum depression. After spending thousands of dollars on infertility diagnosis and treatment, placement fees, and international travel, it can be frightening to realize that being the parent of a child at long last is not "perfect," nor is it the solution to every problem.

Adopters may be afraid to express these feelings to non-adopter friends, believing that they should be blissfully happy to justify the great labors they've undergone. Additionally, the home study process by which adopters are evaluated for our parenting capabilities, can lead adopters to think that they have passed the "test" and will automatically be good parents. But not everyone has top-notch parenting skills; no one is a good parent all of the time. Everyone makes mistakes, yells at their kids, and sometimes uses poor judgment. Don't have unrealistic expectations for either the experience of parenting or for your own parenting skills. You'll have ups and downs like everyone else. Do the best you can, learn from your mistakes, and don't feel guilty. There's no such thing as a perfect parent — biological or adoptive.

c. DEBRIEFING

You have concluded your adoption. It's been finalized in court. Looking back over the past year or longer to when you first looked into adoption you'll find you have come a very long way indeed. You've learned more about adoption, the children who need families, government bureaucracy, police fingerprinting, psychological testing, and the legal process than you knew there was to know. In fact, you're a gold mine of information on how and how not to adopt. Many adoptive parents not only want but need to share their knowledge and experience with others. Of course family and friends will want to hear all about it. Be prepared to tell them all about it, but consider other possibilities too.

(a) Write an article for an adoption periodical. You don't have to be an experienced, published author to write an adoption article. From the glossy national magazines to your local photocopied adoptive parent group newsletter, articles by recent adoptive parents are welcome. Anything of relevance to adoption can be the subject of an article. Many adoption periodicals have writers guidelines you can send for to learn about submission requirements.

(b) Write for non-adoption periodicals. While it may be more difficult to get published in a non-adoption periodical, it can be worthwhile. Your local newspaper may be interested in the story of your adoption. Send a one-page query letter describing the story you plan to write to the community news or Sunday travel section editor and ask if they would be interested in publishing it. Parenting newspapers and magazines published by diaper service companies may also be interested in your story. If you are an experienced writer, you might try a professional market such as a national parenting magazine.

(c) Prepare your child's life book — perhaps the most important and meaningful part of the debriefing process. A life book is the unique record of your child's personal history. You can purchase a "fill-in-the-blanks" life book, but I recommend that you make your own from scratch. It is an enjoyable, creative task and an ongoing one. The easiest format to use is a large three-ring binder that you can add pages to as needed. You may want to organize it like a scrapbook and tape or attach items into the book. You could also use plastic pocket pages into which you can slip fragile items.

What do you include in a life book? You can start with the fact of how your child came to be born, why an adoption plan was made, the story of how your child came into your family, the child's home culture and country if different from yours, who your child is as an individual — personality, looks, interests — and how your family now lives as a unit together. Add pictures of your child's home country, birth family, orphanage, or foster family. Records of all you went through to adopt, including your home study, provide a valuable record and prove to your children just how much you wanted them. Our daughter's life book contains bus tickets, airline menus, photos of her foster family, her home town, and the court hearing. We included our adoption announcement and a narrative to connect all the events together. As we correspond with her foster family, we add their letters to her life book.

Others in the adoption process may want to write something for your child's life book. An orphanage worker, foster parent, counselor, agency social worker, and guardian ad litem could write about how they came to know your child, in the form of a letter to your child or a narrative. If their language is not English, it can be translated later and both versions included in the life book.

Prepare a life book even if there is little information available. If your child has lived in an orphanage, the life book can focus on his or her experience of the place, staff, and other children. However little you have to go on, you know your child is a wonderful, lovable person. You know what your child looks like, enjoys doing, and how your child feels about things.

Adoption professionals feel that however limited or negative the information available, you should nonetheless prepare a life book telling as much as possible without damaging your child's self-esteem. If your daughter was born of rape or incest, to take a worst case example, your life book might start by saying that when her mother gave birth to a wonderful baby, she knew she could not care for her baby in the way she deserved, so she made an adoption plan to give her child the best possible start in life. It is not necessary to say how she was conceived. Remember, it is the *child's* life book. The story should focus on the wonderful baby and what happened to her.

This book may be something your child wishes to share with others at different stages, so be careful to include only facts which you are comfortable with your child knowing or sharing. This doesn't mean, however, that you should keep facts from your children permanently. Private, painful information should be kept confidential and shared with your child at the appropriate time. Most adoption professionals agree that, eventually, adoptees should receive the full story of their adoption.

Older children can participate in making their life book, although that is not mandatory. Helping your children tell their story can be enjoyable and can promote self-esteem. Respect your child's wishes about when and whether to participate in making a life book, but do make one. A child who feels making a life book would bring painful episodes back to life may, someday later, value the life book and be thankful it was made. If you have biological children, consider making a

240

life book for them too. It is a better option than having a single family photo album for biologically related members and a life book only for adoptees. A life book can be a concrete way of helping all children establish a positive identity in their own right. As a side benefit, it can also help you transform your experience into a gift to your child.

d. RECOGNIZING THE CHANGES YOU'VE GONE THROUGH

You have gone through a life-shaping experience. We've looked at ways you can build bridges to the new challenges of parenthood, and how you can debrief and give concrete expression to what you've learned. You have undergone changes and evolution at a personal level as well. Many adopters feels that their experience has made them more sensitive to issues of life and death, poverty, overpopulation, racial prejudice, and a host of social and political problems. Try taking stock of what you have learned and where you have travelled. You will be surprised at how far you have come.

List all the things you learned simply as a result of doing an adoption. Ask yourself: what is the most important lesson your adoption has taught you? Who gave of their time and energy freely to make your adoption happen and why? (Make a list and add up how many names are on it.) What prejudice did you encounter and what did you learn from it? Contrast how you feel about birth parents now with how you felt when you started your adoption. What caused the change? What benefits has your family received that could come to you only through adoption? What was the most difficult thing you had to do to adopt and why? What part of the adoption process was easiest and why? What would you do differently in your adoption if you could do it over and why? If you could give one single piece of advice to would-be adopters, what would it be?

RESOURCE GUIDE

1. Child development books (general)

Faber, Adele and Elaine Mazlish. *Siblings Without Rivalry.* New York: Norton, 1987.

Leach, Penelope. *Your Baby and Child: From Birth to Age Five.* Rev. ed. New York: Knopf, 1989.

White, Burton. *The First Three Years of Life.* Rev. ed. New York: Prentice Hall Press, 1990.

2. Parenting adopted children

Melina, Lois Ruskai. *Making Sense of Adoption: A Parent's Guide.* New York: Harper & Row, 1989.

_____. *Raising Adopted Children.* New York: Harper & Row, 1986.

- *Adopted Child*
  P.O. Box 9362
  Moscow, ID 83843
  (208) 882-1181
  Lois Melina, editor and publisher

3. Resources for locating multicultural toys and books

- Colors of Harmony
  5767 Foster Road
  Bainbridge Island, WA 98110
  1-800-283-5659

- The Heritage Key
  10116 Scoville Avenue
  Sunland, CA 91040
  (818) 951-1438

4. Resources for parenting children of color

Comer, James P. and Alvin F. Poussaint. *Raising Black Children.* New York: Plume Press, 1992.

Powell-Hopson, Darlene and Derke Hopson. *Different and Wonderful: Raising Black Children in a Race Conscious World.* New York: Prentice Hall Press, 1990.

- The National Black Child Development Institute
  1463 Rhode Island Avenue, N.W.
  Washington, D.C. 20005
  (202) 387-1281

5. Books about transracial families and parenting

Gay, Kathlyn. *The Rainbow Effect*. New York: Franklin Watts, 1987.

Root, Maria, ed. *Racially Mixed People in America: Within, Between and Beyond Race*. Newbury Park, CA: Sage Publications, 1992.

Simon, Rita. *Adoption, Race and Identity: From Infancy Through Adolescence*. Westport, CT: Praeger, 1992.

6. Other transracial parenting resources

* *Biracial Child*. The publishers of *Interrace Magazine* are introducing this new periodical in the Fall of 1993. For more information, contact Interrace at P.O. Box 1001, Schenectady, NY 12301, (518) 393-6174.

* *New People*
  P.O. Box 47490
  Oak Park, MI 48237

This bimonthly periodical addresses social, legal, legislative, parenting, and education issues of interest to multiracial/interracial families. It also sponsors an annual convention.

* *Pact Press*
  3315 Sacramento Street, Suite 239
  San Francisco, CA 94118

This quarterly, focusing on raising adopted children of color, contains articles by adoption professionals and all triad members.

Ramos, Joan D. *Multicultural Resources for Adoptive Families*. Seattle, WA: Children's Home Society, 1992.

To obtain this free guide write to: Adoption Resource Center, Children's Home Society, 3300 N.E. 65th Street, Seattle, WA 98115-0190

7. Resources for parenting older and special needs children

Fahlberg, Vera. *A Child's Journey Through Placement*. Indianapolis, IN: Perspectives Press, 1991.

Jewett, Claudia. *Helping Children Cope with Separation and Loss*. Boston, MA: Harvard Common Press, 1978.

* National Foster Parents Association (see chapter 5 Resource Guide.)

* National Information Center for Children and Youth with Disabilities (NICHCY)
  P.O. Box 1492
  Washington, DC 20013
  1-800-999-5599; (703) 893-8614

- People of Every Stripe!
  Galleria — 3rd Floor
  921 S.W. Morrison
  Portland, OR 97205
  (503) 224-8057

Soft dolls who have disabilities as well as dolls of different racial and ethnic heritage can be ordered. All can be customized.

Books about adoption

Hundreds of books have been written about adoption for children. The best way to investigate them is to look up one of the extensive bibliographies of adoption literature for children. *Ours* Magazine (see chapter 1 Resource Guide) and *Adopted Child* publish such bibliographies. The one listed below also includes books which, while not about adoption, feature characters who have been adopted. And don't forget classics such as *Anne of Green Gables, Daddy Long Legs,* and *The Wizard of Oz.*

Miles, Susan G. *Adoption Literature for Children and Young Adults: An Annotated Bibliography.* Westport, CT: Greenwood Press, 1991.

TIPS

You and your children are bound to come across books that show adoption in a negative or pejorative light. These attitudes are pervasive and your children will eventually come into contact with people who share these views, no matter how carefully you try to protect them. You can use such unpleasant discoveries as an opportunity to discuss negative adoption stereotypes with your child, note that prejudiced attitudes may come up in books and conversation, and rehearse a response that your child can give when confronted with these views. Being prepared to encounter prejudice is an important tool in combating it. Children who are protected from negative views on adoption may be unprepared when exposed to them outside the home.

14
BECOMING A COMMUNITY RESOURCE

Becoming a community resource is a multi-level process. Each level leads to the next and integrates what you have learned from the previous stages, as adoption professional, Judith Anderson, has observed. At first, the task is to identify what it is you have to share, such as your adoptive experience and personal attributes — your background, education, professional, and volunteer experience. The second step is finding a way to share your experience with others, such as teaching a class, volunteering, or acting as a resource person for a group. At the third level you use your experience in a more formal way. You advocate for legislative and social change and participate in efforts to bring about needed improvements. Finally, you evolve into an expert yourself. You are the person decision-makers turn to when they want to consult a particular constituency. They ask you for help.

a. VOLUNTEERING: SHARING YOUR EXPERIENCE WITH OTHERS

Probably the most useful contribution you can make is to offer to share your hard-won expertise with others seeking to adopt. Your adoptive parent group may operate an information referral service in which callers are referred to adopters with a particular kind of experience. If you adopted independently, for example, you could discuss the steps you went through with callers considering independent adoption. Your adoption agency may also appreciate your offer to speak with clients considering adoption through them, not only to give an agency character reference, but to share the ins and outs of the experience. See chapter 14 for additional ideas. Some adopters feel that after years of focusing on adoption, they need to look elsewhere for a change. Someone who adopted in Guatemala could volunteer with an aid organization that provides food and medical care to Guatemalan children. Helping in a play group for special needs children would be another choice. There are many applications for the skills adopters acquire in the course of becoming parents.

b. ADVOCATING FOR CHANGE: USING YOUR KNOWLEDGE SYSTEMATICALLY

As an adoptive parent, you now know more about adoption than most people, not to mention a lot about parenting as well. If you are parenting a stepchild or relative, you have firsthand knowledge of issues confronting today's fragmented North American family. We have seen how you can share information with people who seek to do what you have successfully carried out. Your expertise can also be a valuable community resource at another level.

You know that adoption can be too expensive, that although non-traditional families can make fine parents they still encounter many roadblocks to adoption. You may have discovered facilitators or agencies operating unethically while you were evaluating your options. Your trip to South America may have drawn your attention to economic and social injustice in another society. Now is the time to consider working together with others to bring about change.

There are organizations that lobby for legislative change at local, state, and federal levels. Adoptive parents have been at the forefront of groups seeking to pass a tax deduction for adoption expenses. Others have joined with adoptees and birth parents to make access to birth records less burdensome. The official U.S. delegation to the Hague Convention included adoptive parent representatives.

246

Not every position taken by adoptive parent groups and individuals will conform with your own views, of course. But if you feel strongly about an adoption-related issue, consider lending your voice to changing the status quo. Join an organization and work to reform the law — that's how laws get passed! Recognize your expertise and trade on it. You can make a real difference if you choose.

c. BECOMING A RESOURCE FOR DECISION-MAKERS

Through your advocacy efforts, you can be certain that community leaders will learn of your existence. You may become a leader yourself. As you acquire volunteer expertise and confidence, you will find that people turn to you for help. You may be asked to participate in adoption conferences as a workshop leader or to teach a community college class. There are many possibilities, from developing advocacy into a career to running for public office. Adopters have successfully done all these and more.

d. WHERE TO START LOOKING FOR ADVOCACY OPPORTUNITIES

Your first step is to consider what you would enjoy doing. There are abundant opportunities for advocacy in many areas. The great thing about volunteering is that it's voluntary. The work should be meaningful, enjoyable, and challenging. If not, there are plenty of opportunities to volunteer elsewhere.

1. Metropolitan areas

Opportunities are abundant in metropolitan areas. If you want to stick with adoption advocacy, contact adoptive family groups and adoption agencies and ask if they need a willing volunteer. Outside of adoption, groups work with homeless children, with runaways, or they support low-income families through food banks and clothing drives.

Within political parties, if you are in one or wish to join, there are usually groups or committees who work to formulate policies on issues relating to children, and you may be able to offer your services there. If you are interested in legislative change, you'll find that many adoption groups have active legislative committees that will welcome your participation.

2. Smaller communities and rural areas

If you live in a small or sparsely populated community, your task will be more challenging. At the same time, opportunities may be easier to grasp since there will be fewer people involved. If your community has no adoptive parent support group, consider starting one. You may have to cast your net over a wide area, but there are probably more adoptive parents than you think in your community. If you are a non-relative adopter, consider inviting stepparents and relative adopters to join your group. These constituencies are often left out of adoption groups.

Your group doesn't have to be large; a few enthusiastic families can do a lot. You can form a play group, discuss parenting issues, and develop community adoption celebrations. Even small communities have children who need families. Your local public agency may have suggestions for volunteering. Your local church is another source of volunteer opportunities.

If you have a computer and modem, you can join the brave new world of computer bulletin boards and electronic mail. Communicate with groups and individuals thousands of miles away and share ideas and experience. If you belong to a home computer user network such as Compuserv, America On line, or Prodigy, you may be able to find like-minded individuals who have adopted or who share a desire to advocate for children.

3. Internationally

Millions of the world's children die each year of preventable diseases such as measles, polio, dysentery, cholera, diphtheria, and typhoid. Adoption does not really address these problems in a significant way. It allows us to become parents and our children to grow up in affluent families. It does nothing in and of itself to remedy dire conditions in the child's birth country.

Most parents in developing countries who place children for adoption would not dream of doing so if they weren't desperate. Grateful for the opportunity to parent our wonderful children, many adopters feel that we owe a debt to the society that gave them to us and seek a way to improve life for families there before adoption is considered. Working toward such a goal also demonstrates to our children that we respect and value their heritage and are prepared to work to preserve it.

Some adoption agencies operate aid programs. These range from orphanages to programs that supply medical supplies, clothing, and food to families abroad. Famine relief organizations operate programs worldwide and the United Nations also sponsors programs to improve the status of children. Churches have extensive programs throughout the world to aid children and families. Amnesty organizations work to free political prisoners and restore respect for human rights in many countries. You could call or write to one of the organizations in the chapter 3 Resource Guide and ask for opportunities to volunteer.

4. Person to person

At an individual level, you are now an adoption advocate. When you hear disparaging remarks about adoption and people of other races and cultures, take the opportunity to gently educate those who make such remarks and explain why they are misguided. If you don't get anywhere, you can still let them know that you will not tolerate remarks like

"Couldn't you have one of your own?" or "What happened to her real mother?" Usually, such statements are not consciously intended to hurt, but the speaker needs to be shown how and why it is inappropriate. Personal questions about your child's heritage and family background in your child's presence may also be inappropriate. You are now a member of a minority group (if you weren't one already): adoptive parents. You may wish to read about discrimination, stereotyping, and how they affect us if this is a new experience for you. Remember, you are your child's advocate and you represent adoptive families to many non-adopters. Taking a stand to affirm your values and your legitimacy as a family can be empowering for you and educational for those who come in contact with you. This is a valid and important form of advocacy.

5. Group to group

An adoptive parent group can form coalitions with other groups. Issues such as obtaining tax benefits for adoptive families, rewriting government forms to reflect modern multiracial and interracial realities, and opening adoption records have been tackled by coalitions of groups including adoptive families, birth parents and adult adoptees, adoption professionals, foster families, and organizations that promote racial equality. An umbrella organization that represents many times more people in a much larger geographical area and from a wider variety of backgrounds than a single group can be an effective tool. You can also pool resources and share tasks such as contacting legislators and preparing a media campaign more effectively if there are more of you.

6. Group to decision-makers

Formal advocacy is an art. If your organization wants to persuade decision-makers to do something, community resources exist to teach you how to advocate effectively. The Public Interest Research Group in Washington, D.C. and many affiliated local groups offer information and workshops to consumer and other advocacy groups on lobbying, conducting media campaigns, and coalition building. Advocacy training is sometimes offered through churches and community help organizations.

One often overlooked source of expertise in this area is the staff of elected representatives. These people deal with the public every day, answer letters from constituents, and listen to lobbyists. They have the ear of their boss and they also know what the forces are opposed to and in favor of an issue. You can call your local constituency office and speak with your representative's assistant to discuss an issue of importance to you. Once you have an issue you are pursuing, these staff people are your connection to the decision-maker. Learn who they are, treat them with consideration, and they can help you to put forward your agenda effectively.

If your group is willing to serve as an adviser to decision-makers, let them know this. Write a letter to government and business leaders stating who you represent and that you are willing to offer your expertise and opinion on adoption issues.

RESOURCE GUIDE

1. Resources for community advocates

- American Self Help Clearinghouse
  St. Clares — Riverside Medical Center
  Denville, NJ 07834
  (201) 625-7101
  TDD (201) 625-9053; FAX 625-8848

- The National Committee for Citizens in Education
  900 — 2nd Street NE, Suite 8
  Washington, DC 20002
  (202) 408-0447

- National Healthlines Directory
  Information Resources Press
  1110 North Glebe Road
  Arlington, VA 22201
  (703) 558-8270

251

- Public Interest Research Group
  National Lobbying Office
  215 Pennsylvania Avenue S.E.
  Washington, DC 20003
  (202) 546-9707

2. Books about the need for advocacy and how to do it

Edelman, Marian Wright. *The Measure of Our Success: A Letter to My Children and Yours.* Boston, MA: Beacon Press, 1992

Lewis, Barbara A. *The Kids' Guide to Social Action: How to Solve the Social Problems You Choose and Turn Creative Thinking into Positive Action.* Minneapolis, MN: Free Spirit Publishing, Inc., 1991.

Walls, David. *The Activist's Almanac: The Concerned Citizen's Guide to the Leading Advocacy Organizations in America.* New York: Simon & Schuster, 1993.

Wilson, Marlene. *You Can Make a Difference! Helping Others and Yourself Through Volunteering.* Boulder, CO: Volunteer Management Associates, 1990.

TIPS

See the Resource Guides for chapters 1, 3, 5, 12 and 13 for lists of organizations which welcome volunteers from the adoption community. If you are interested in the issue of adoptee rights, several nationwide organizations which exist to advocate for adoptees and issues which concern them welcome volunteers.

Advocates for Open Records and Search and Reunion Groups

- Adoptees Liberation Movement Association Reunion Registry
  P.O. Box 727
  Radio City Station
  New York, NY 10101-0727
  (212) 581-1568

- American Adoption Congress
  P.O. Box 44040
  L'Enfant Plaza
  Washington, DC 20026-0040

- Council for Equal Rights in Adoption (CERA)
  401 E. 74th Street, Suite 17D
  New York, NY 10021
  (212) 988-0110

GLOSSARY OF
ADOPTION TERMINOLOGY*

ABANDON

To leave behind, to cease taking responsibility for. Unfortunately, some people assume that all adopted children have been abandoned by their birth parents. In fact, it is rare for an adopted child anywhere to have been abandoned. Children whose parents are desperate may leave them on a doorstep, but that doorstep was chosen to ensure that someone would find and care for the child. Children may be left with nurses in hospitals for the same reason. In rare instances of true abandonment, a child is left with disregard for whether he or she will survive.

ADOPT

To become the legal parents of a child or adult; to assert ownership of or control over something already in existence. This term has become popular in a fundraising context, as in "adopt-a-highway" or "adopt-a-zoo-animal" programs. Many in the adoption community feel this use of "adopt" demeans children and families touched by adoption. It also subtly perpetuates the "rescue" image of adoption that distorts the motivations and values inherent in adoption.

ADOPTEE/ADOPTED CHILD

Child who has been legally adopted. This term is fine to use when it is necessary to distinguish between adopted and

---

*Adoption terminology is changing. New terminology to give a more accurate and positive picture of adoption today is called "positive adoption language." Some terms are universally accepted within the adoption community; others are controversial. This glossary covers most of the terms commonly used in adoption. Where there is disagreement on a term, alternatives are given.

biological children, or to discuss issues that pertain only to those who have been adopted. However, once your adopted child is in your home, he or she is your child, period. Many adoptive parents cringe when asked "Which one is your adopted child?" We find we must make the point gently that the common denominator in our families is that our children are simply that — our children.

ADOPTION PLAN (make an adoption plan/choose adoption)

The arrangement made by birth parents, adoptive parents, and intermediaries providing who will take responsibility for parenting a child. Some in the adoption community feel this term should be used for all adoptions; others feel it is only appropriate if a plan was actually made.

ADOPTION TRIAD

Birth parents, adoptive parents, and adopted child. The use of this term, preferred over "adoption triangle" excludes others directly affected by adoption such as biological children of both sets of parents.

BIOLOGICAL/BIOLOGIC PARENT

The parent who provided the genetic material to conceive a child. A semen or egg donor is a biological parent of a child born from the donation. A woman who gestates a fetus for other biological parents of the same child may or may not be a biological parent by law. The matter is under litigation.

BIRACIAL

Children whose parents are of two different races.
See also "multiracial."

BIRTH FATHER

The biological father of an adopted child. Today, birth fathers play an increasingly important role in adoption plans for their children. The emotional consequences and losses of adoption are increasingly understood to affect both parents.

BIRTH MOTHER

The biological mother of an adopted child. The unwieldy term, "woman in whose body you grew" has, fortunately, not gained much of a following. This appears to be a misguided attempt to refrain from using the word "mother" in connection with a birth mother. Most in the adoption community feel that "birth mother" is the better description. As a way of describing a birth mother to a young child, "the mommy in whose tummy you grew" is likely to be less frightening than the implication that the birth mother is an alien woman with no "momminess" about her.

CHILD OF YOUR OWN

This is a term directed at adoptive parents by others to describe a child who was not adopted, often to ask if they have or could have such a child. One response adopters give when this remark is directed at them is "But (my adopted child) is my own."

CHILDFREE (to live childfree)

Live without biological or adopted children. This is the term preferred by infertile people who have chosen to end infertility treatment or other pursuits of parenthood and live without biological or adopted children. The term is generally construed as a step forward. It is not always favored by those not yet resolved in infertility, or for preferential adopters. Some feel the term has a "pest-free" connotation, which suggests that children are pests. Whatever it is called, the childfree movement has provided a positive model for those stuck on the infertility treadmill.

CLOSED ADOPTION/OPEN ADOPTION

An adoption in which birth and adoptive parents and child are given no identifying information about one another. An adoption in which birth and adoptive families meet, but do not exchange identifying information, and contact is mediated by a third party is "semi-closed" or "semi-open." An adoption in which birth and adoptive families can identify one another and make contact without requring third party intervention is open.

CULTURE/ETHNICITY

Groupings of people by certain characteristics, such as country or region of origin, or historical tradition. Culture and ethnicity both fall short of racial distinctions, but imply more than belonging to a religion or favoring a particular style of dress. Several cultures and ethnic groups may exist within a single society. The Gypsy population of Romania is an ethnic group; Irish Canadians are as well.

DECIDED TO KEEP

Where a birth parent decides against adoption and chooses to parent the child instead. There is nothing terribly negative about this term except for the fact that it implies a child is an object to own, keep, or give away. Historically, children have been viewed as chattel. In today's world, terms that imply ownership of human beings are frowned on. "Decided to parent" is the preferred term.

HARD-TO-PLACE/SPECIAL NEEDS

Children for whom families are not easily found because the children have special needs or traits that make parenting them a more challenging task than parenting a healthy newborn. "Hard-to-place" is giving way to the more popular "special needs." The term "special needs" also covers children whose only true special need is for a family — such as older children of color and sibling groups of all races.

HOME STUDY

The pre-placement or pre-finalization report required to be submitted to the court with jurisdiction over adoption, it must contain a positive recommendation of the adopters and other information as required by the state where the adoption occurs and/or another state or country, if involved. No one is happy with this term, but no universally accepted replacement has been found. Some prefer "pre-placement report," and writer Patricia Irwin Johnston has suggested "parent preparation" as a more "user friendly" term. However, while some agencies provide parent preparation along with a home study, others do not. The state-mandated content of the home study, criminal background check and financial statement, and the fact that new home studies are required for even the most experienced and "prepared" repeat adopters indicate that its purpose is still a threshhold test of adopter worthiness.

ILLEGITIMATE

A child born out of wedlock (antiquated). This term no longer accurately describes a child born out of wedlock in Canada or the United States. It dates from a time when children born out of wedlock could not inherit from the estate of a deceased biological parent.

INTERNATIONAL/INTERCOUNTRY ADOPTION

An adoption in which a child born in one country is adopted by parents in another country. Either of these terms is appropriate. The Hague Convention uses "intercountry." "Foreign adoption" is not acceptable, since "foreign" has a connotation of alien or strange.

LEGAL GUARDIANSHIP

A form of custody arrangement which can be made for children, or for adults who are not mentally competent. It confers the power to make parenting decisions, but does not sever biological ties.

MULTIRACIAL (multicultural/multiethnic)

Partaking of more than one race, culture, or ethnicity.

NATURAL PARENT

Biological parent of a child. This unfortunate term is still in common use by the media and the public. It implies that non-biological parents are "unnatural" or "artificial." Although at one time, "natural" meant "of biological origin," today it has come to mean "normal," while "unnatural" means "strange, wrong." Efforts to impose positive adoption language notwithstanding, "natural parent" shows no signs of disappearing yet.

PLACE A CHILD

To make an adoption plan for a child, to move a child to the home of adoptive parents as the result of an adoption plan or involuntary termination of parent rights. This term is largely accepted within the adoption community, although some feel that it has a connotation of ownership and objectifies the child.

POSITIVE ADOPTION LANGUAGE (P.A.L.)

Adoption terminology that casts adoption in a positive rather than a negative light.

PUT UP FOR ADOPTION

To place for adoption. This term comes from several sources. The earliest usage was "put out/put up for indenture." Later in the mid-19th century, thousands of orphans sent by train to the Midwest were "put up" for adoption on train platforms and town halls. Both origins reflect the sad history of adoption, not the current reality.

RACE

People who share certain genetically transmitted physical characteristics that are not common to all human beings. This definition is unsatisfactory, if scientifically accurate. While so-called racial characteristics may or may not be obvious, in our society we tend to view race as always a visible distinction. "Race" is rarely used scientifically in our society.

REAL PARENT

Out-of-favor term for biological parent.

RELINQUISH/SURRENDER (a child for adoption)

Where a birth parent accepts without opposition the termination of parental rights. Both these terms are preferable to "give up," "give away," or "put up" for adoption. They define without an emotional subtext what is actually occurring. The other terms imply the birth parent does not care what happens to the child. But where a mother makes an adoption plan, "relinquish" and "surrender" are not appropriate, as they describe a reaction to a plan made by others, not by the birth mother herself.

REUNION

The meeting of biological parent(s) and their child placed for adoption. This term is controversial. Many adoptive parents prefer "meeting" or "contact" because "reunion" implies a coming together at which people are reunited for future togetherness. Since few adoptees and birth parents meet in order to reestablish a parent-child relationship, "reunion" is inappropriate. However, others feel "reunion" is appropriate because it conveys more emotion than "meeting," which may apply just as easily to business gatherings.

SEARCH

For an adoptee to seek to identify and sometimes (although not always) to establish contact with one or more birth parents.

TRANSRACIAL ADOPTION

Adoption of a child of one or more races by parent(s) of one or more different races from that of the child. "Interracial adoption" is also acceptable, but less used. Interestingly, our views of race, often unscientific, color whether an adoption is seen as transracial. Children of Latino descent may be seen as transracial adoptees, although they are technically of the same race as the adoptive parents.

OTHER TITLES IN THE SELF-COUNSEL SERIES

START AND RUN A PROFITABLE HOME DAY CARE
Your step-by-step business plan
by Catherine Pruissen

Here is a book for all those whose love of children is matched by the desire to be their own boss. It shows exactly what it takes to start a home-based day care and run it as a money-making business.

Author Catherine Pruissen guides readers through the start-up stage and well beyond. She describes the qualities an owner needs as he or she becomes everything from the bookkeeper to the storyteller. Her book details how to get all the licenses a center must obtain, how to meet health and safety standards, and what equipment it must have. It also shows how to successfully market the service and handle all the day-to-day and long-range operations.

Day care is a growth industry. Parents will pay a premium to make sure their child has a place in a safe and nurturing day care. This book is the perfect resource for those who want to establish themselves as child care professionals, not just babysitters. $14.95

BIRTH ORDER AND YOU
How your sex and position in the family affects your personality and relationships
by Dr. Ron Richardson and Lois A. Richardson, M.A.

Are you the oldest, middle, or youngest child in your family? Are you a leader or a follower? An introvert or an extrovert? Your position in the family has a far-reaching effect on the way you experience the world — it is a cornerstone of your personality. With insight and accuracy, this book shows you the way to a greater understanding of your friends, family, and yourself. $7.95

Some of the topics covered are:

- Why birth order matters
- How the sex of your siblings affects your personality
- Introducing birth order position and sex
- Oldest children
- Youngest children
- Middle children
- Only children
- Twins
- Exceptions and variations: Factors that alter the usual birth order pattern
- Parenting your children of different birth orders
- Siblings as a psychological resource

ORDER FORM

All prices are subject to change without notice. Books are available in book, department, and stationery stores. If you cannot buy the book through a store, please use this order form. (Please print)

Name _____

Address _____

_____

Charge to: ❑Visa   ❑ MasterCard

Account Number _____

Validation Date _____

Expiry Date_____

Signature_____

❑Check here for a free catalogue.

IN CANADA
Please send your order to the nearest location:
Self-Counsel Press
1481 Charlotte Road
North Vancouver, B. C.
V7J 1H1
Self-Counsel Press
8-2283 Argentia Road
Mississauga, Ontario
L5N 5Z2
IN THE U.S.A.
Please send your order to:
Self-Counsel Press Inc.
1704 N. State Street
Bellingham, WA 98225

YES, please send me:

_____copies of **Start and Run a Profitable Home Day Care**, $14.95

_____copies of **Birth Order and You**, $7.95

Please add $2.50 for postage & handling.
Canadian residents, please add 7% GST to your order.
WA residents, please add 7.8% sales tax.